PHILOSOPHY
50 KEY IDEAS UNPACKED

PHILOSOPHY
50 KEY IDEAS UNPACKED

MICHAEL MOORE

This edition published in 2023 by Arcturus Publishing Limited
26/27 Bickels Yard, 151–153 Bermondsey Street,
London SE1 3HA

AD011246US

Printed in the UK

Contents

Introduction

The aim of this book is to focus on 50 important philosophical ideas. The insight required of the philosophers who came up with these profound, wholly inventive, and influential ideas is nothing short of astonishing: this is a book that took centuries and lifetimes to write. The ideas that appear on these pages are the culmination of thinkers who have spent their lives and energy thinking about the realities surrounding human life and knowledge. In turn these thinkers were often, if not always, reacting to and further developing ideas that they had read, spoken, and thought about. Now this conversation, which is itself the heart of philosophical practice, has come to you.

An appreciation of the laborious origin of these ideas is important for several reasons. No book can claim to include all the ideas worthy of philosophical merit without running to volumes. But the virtue of limiting ourselves to 50 ideas, spanning the beginning of philosophy in

The School of Athens *by Raphael depicts many of the most important philosophers in history, with Plato and Aristotle in discussion at the center of the image.*

Ancient Greece to the present time, is that all the ideas are brilliant and interesting. A second reason for acknowledging the pioneering excellence of these philosophers is that the ideas presented here might take some careful thought on your part. I have attempted to summarize complex ideas so that they are simplified and clarified, but full comprehension will demand a little work from you. Sometimes it will require a pause to digest an idea or reread a section. In recompense there are few intellectual tasks as rewarding as understanding an idea, the very same idea that was in the mind of Aristotle or René Descartes.

The pleasure of this book, like all books, is not in merely reading, but in reading and understanding. With this in mind the chapters are short and digestible, and illustrations of various kinds have been added to the text to aid in achieving this understanding. So pay attention to these aids as they appear in the book. More than any other book, it is true to say of a book of philosophy that if you are not understanding, you are not enjoying the text.

The scope of the chapters is broadly chronological, with roughly the first third of the book devoted to ancient philosophy and the last third comprising ideas from early modern philosophy to the current day. In the middle are chapters concerned with broader concepts such as Good and Evil or the Existence of God.

As for the ideas themselves, some ideas represent the absolute core of a philosopher's thinking, such as Aristotle's Four Causes (see page 59) or Kierkegaard's Three Stages on Life's Way (see page 109). Yet others represent a philosophical puzzle such as Newcomb's Paradox (see page 189) or Gettier Problems (see page 159). This is not to establish a judgment of value or worth, only to note that different ideas have different contexts, goals, and scope.

As you read, you will see that the idea of an idea is itself a bit of a philosophical conundrum. Many ideas are self-contained and easily expressible as such—for example, one of Zeno's paradoxes that motion is impossible. However, a great many philosophical ideas are themselves dependent on and interconnected with other ideas. It is impossible to speak of Nietzsche's Superman without talking about the *will to power*, or *herd mentality*, or the *death of God*; for all these ideas are central to rightly comprehending the Superman.

Lastly, it is for this same reason that many of the chapters have at least partial similarity to other chapters. So Aristotle's Categories are in a sense that philosopher's answer to Plato's Forms, and Descartes's *Cogito Ergo Sum* is a reply to the Pyrrhonian attack seen in the Skeptical Outlook. In short, the history of ideas is interconnected, and ideas will influence other ideas, including your own.

1

The Chief Good or Purpose for Mankind

What is the chief purpose for mankind? This is probably the most important question that can be asked, for it affects our happiness, our actions, and our future. In Ancient Greece this was a topic of great interest and manifested in disputes and rivalry among different philosophical schools, which each construed the purpose differently.

In general terms they talked about this purpose as the *telos*, a Greek word for "end" or "goal," introduced into ethical theory by Aristotle (384–322 BCE). The goal of life differed, but there was at least a consensus, an assumption, that there was a purpose for life, a final goal to which we should order our whole lives. The idea of this *telos* is not about some vague hope for the future, but rather makes demands on how we ought to live now. The chief purpose is not just a guiding light or a suggestion; it is *the* Good.

THE EPICUREAN APPROACH

The most controversial of the schools was the Epicurean school, for they considered pleasure to be the chief purpose. There are few who deny that pleasure is good, or at least can be a good, but the Epicurean insistence on the primacy of pleasure led to charges of sensual indulgence and immoral living. One of the consequences of positing a chief good is that anything except the chief good can be used in order to attain it. In the case of the Epicureans, this not only leads to downplaying what to others seem like good things, but sometimes choosing what seems bad in itself in order to attain the chief good. So the Epicureans were accused of ignoring virtues and even sometimes embracing what is shameful in their pursuit of pleasure.

THE STOIC APPROACH

The Stoics serve as a good contrast to the claims of the Epicurean school. For, instead of pleasure, they held that virtue was not only the chief good but the only good. There are two significant effects of this belief. The first is that it is possible to attain happiness with virtue alone, despite whatever difficult or even horrendous personal circumstances you are in, such as extreme poverty or disease. If nothing can change the independence of virtue by taking away from its goodness, it follows that neither can anything be added. So for the Stoics, virtue plus money or virtue plus good looks was just as good as virtue by itself.

As Stoics and Epicureans posited radically different conceptions of the chief good, so too did they maintain a bitter philosophical rivalry. Part of the dispute involved seeking common ground from which to proceed. The concept of nature was one such starting point held in common. The Epicureans and Stoics each believed that nature was on their side. The Epicureans said that nature shows children and young animals seeking pleasure from the moment they are born, while the Stoics claimed that self-preservation, which leads to virtue, is what is actually seen in the young.

THE PERIPATETIC SCHOOL

The Peripatetic school, named for Aristotle's habit of walking while teaching, held a more capacious view of the chief good, regardless of whether it is more or less compelling. Aristotle believed that the goal of human life was happiness itself, understood as a whole life lived virtuously in accordance with reason. But the concept of a "whole life" is doing more here than just emphasizing duration. It includes a number of subsidiary good things like friendship, health, and adequate financial means, all established within the context of a city, or at least a community, of similarly virtuous residents. So Aristotle would agree with the Stoics that virtue is something highly desirable, while insisting that it must be attended with other external goods. For Aristotle pleasure is highly desirable, but it is a natural effect of seeking and attaining what is actually good.

THE PLATONIC APPROACH

With Plato (428–348 BCE) we have a conception of the chief good that is the most simple but also the most abstract. Like Aristotle, he was committed to a belief in happiness and insisted that virtue was the

The Chief Good

way to attain this happiness. Happiness is achieved by an orientation involving a life of inquiry and, above all, an examination of the self. This is the source of the Socratic ethos that an unexamined life is not worth living. Knowledge for Plato is tightly aligned with happiness; in some places he strongly implies that knowledge alone is sufficient to account for virtue and for happiness as well. The ultimate good is not something mundane like pleasure, which he thinks is the cause of many evils, or even friends, who will eventually pass away. The ultimate goal of our mortal concerns should be the Form of the Good. Plato does not tell us much about this mysterious entity. But it plays a central role in his philosophy, for it is because of the Form of the Good that all other good things are good. Even virtues themselves gain their goodness from this Good. It so transcends our known experience that Plato says it is even "beyond being."

THE PYRRHONIAN APPROACH

In light of the various candidates for the chief good, you might well be conflicted or confused about which is the best. One of the later

Greek philosophical schools, the Pyrrhonian Skeptics, seemed to share this perplexity at competing claims from Aristotelian Peripatetics, Platonists, Stoics, and Epicureans. The Platonists have a wholly transcendent chief good, while the Epicureans have an all too familiar good: pleasure. The Skeptics believed that all this disputation and thinking about the chief good actually inhibits rather than leads to happiness. The goal or

Aristotle introduced the idea of the telos, *the chief goal to which people should direct their actions. The purpose of philosophy was to help determine what this* telos *should be.*

chief good, paradoxically, is for the Skeptic to refrain from trying to determine the chief good. The chief good is to be in a state of tranquility (Greek *ataraxia*). The way to secure this tranquility is to refrain from having beliefs of any kind, for beliefs can lead only to disturbance, the enemy of happiness.

School	Chief Good
Epicureanism	Pleasure
Stoicism	Virtue alone
Aristotelianism	Virtue + external + internal goods
Platonism	Knowledge of the Forms and the Form of the Good
Pyrrhonian Skepticism	Tranquility

2

Determinism and Free Will

Love, career, friends, beliefs, leisure, and more or less every significant and meaningful action in our lives seems to be a matter of choice. But what if our lives and the choices that make up our lives are decided not by us but by something or someone else?

Aristotle's sea battle

It is true or false *right now* that there will be a sea battle tomorrow.

If it is true *right now*—it has been predetermined that there will be a sea battle.

We would undoubtedly like to know if this is the case. Or would we? If we are predetermined to act and choose as we do, do we want to know? If there is a God or gods, are they pulling the strings of our lives?

ARISTOTLE AND HIS REJECTION OF DETERMINISM

Considerations such as these led Aristotle (384–322 BCE) to make a distinction between the future and our thoughts about the future. He wanted to deny that determinism—the belief that the future has been determined and is inevitable—is true. A general observation he makes on the question of determinism is that we think about a course of action only when we think it is within our power to affect it for the better. On the other hand, we do not deliberate about those things we have no ability to change. We do not deliberate about whether the sun will rise tomorrow. We can think about this, but we do not deliberate about it because we do not have the ability to influence it. We can think about it, or even hope that it comes about, but we reserve deliberation for a course of action that we, as personal agents, can bring about.

A second point of Aristotle is that statements about the future are either true or false, just as in a general way every statement is either

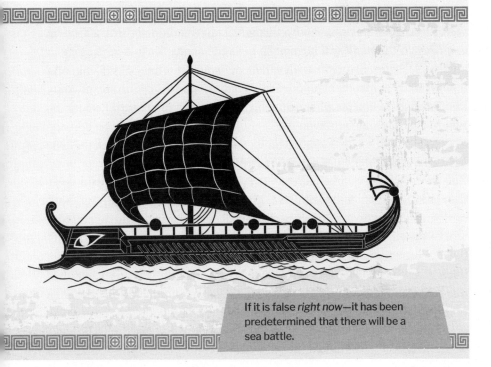

If it is false *right now*—it has been predetermined that there will be a sea battle.

true or false. He gives an example of a sea battle, saying "There will be a sea battle tomorrow." If this is true or false, then it is true or false *right now*. If it is true right now that there will be a sea battle tomorrow, it seems it is the case that the sea battle is necessary. Granting necessity to the sea battle is no different from saying that the sea battle has been determined ahead of time. In addition, the past cannot be changed. So if it was true in the past that the sea battle would occur, then this cannot change in future, since to do so would be to change the past and the past cannot change. One clever suggestion offered to us by Aristotle is that just as the past cannot change so also the present cannot change. If you are reading this right now, it is true you are reading and impossible that you are not reading at this very moment. If something is occurring at this very moment, we seem to have direct agency over the outcome compared to the past or future.

In addition to more abstract considerations over the nature of necessity and fate, there is also the human side of the equation. Aristotle discussed voluntary actions and defined them as those in which we make a decision not clouded by ignorance and chosen according to some internal principle, such as a belief. An involuntary action is one which is out of our control, such as a sailor being swept out to sea by a strong storm. Some actions can be, in a limited sense, both voluntary and involuntary, so Aristotle calls these mixed. A sailor who throws cargo overboard during a storm to preserve the boat and human lives is his example. It is voluntary in that the sailor performs it with full knowledge of what he is doing, and it is involuntary in that the particular circumstances of the storm draw him towards a course of action (throwing cargo overboard) which he would not normally choose.

THE STOICS' EMBRACE OF DETERMINISM

The Stoic school of philosophy, unlike Aristotle, believed in a view that today we call compatibilism. This is the belief that things are both determined and are voluntarily chosen. To understand how this feature worked itself out in the everyday occurrence of choice, we need to clarify two further Stoic doctrines. One is the idea of an individual nature. Each of us has a character or nature which is truly ours as a result of our moral education and choices. The other relevant aspect is the idea of impressions. For the Stoics an impression is anything that appears to be desirable, or not, for one reason or another. A hot bowl of soup or a warm inviting bed after a long day are two examples. The soup gives the impression of tastiness and so we take up the action of eating it. It was in our power to refuse the soup, but once we have begun eating the soup there is a sense in which the soup causes us to be as we are: on the biological level to enjoy and digest the soup, on the psychological level perhaps to continue eating and think about the soup. Our reaction to the soup is a reflection of our nature or character, so that in one sense our reaction to the soup is because of who we are and so voluntary, and involuntary in that the soup is making our character behave in a certain way.

A fascinating illustration of this Stoic conception of free will is a cylindrical stone on a hill. It sits there at the top of the hill and someone or something pushes it. Take this push to be analogous to an impression, such as getting a glance at desirable soup. After this slight push, the cylinder gets going faster and faster downhill. The initial push came from outside, but its impact is negligible, as most of the movement comes from the stone itself, in its momentum from its round nature. Likewise, although we are prodded by impressions, it is our own natures that determine the lion's share of our actions.

The Stoic conception of free will

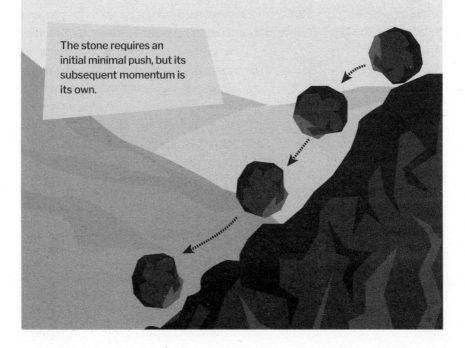

The stone requires an initial minimal push, but its subsequent momentum is its own.

3

Zeno's Paradoxes – The Impossibility of Motion and Change

Only a madman would deny there is motion in the universe. Trains, cars, bees, birds, dogs, and clouds are just a few of the things that move. There is an endless parade of movement before us every day. Yet Zeno of Elea (495–430 BCE) denied this very thing.

In doing so, he was attempting to defend the idea of his mentor, Parmenides (fl. 475 BCE), that the universe is one. Zeno believed that if the concept of motion were permitted, this would leave space for a multiplicity of things, since motion is a kind of change, and a change requires differences. In order to argue against motion, Zeno came up with paradoxes that he believed showed the impossibility of motion. These paradoxes were not designed to argue for the singularity of the universe. Rather, Zeno intended for them a purely refutative role, to show that the multiplicity of the universe was an absurdity.

Zeno of Elea introduced some of the most well-known paradoxes of philosophy, such as the Arrow Paradox and Achilles and the Tortoise.

THE ARROW PARADOX

Probably the least convincing of Zeno's proofs for non-motion involves an arrow. This idea requires that we conceive of time as a chain of connected present moments. Time is conceived as the collection of these present moments, and so if motion is going to occur, it must occur within time, construed as the present in some sense. Because something, in this case an arrow, is in a present "now," the arrow is not moving, because the now is not moving—the now is here and now, not going into the future and it has already emerged from the past. It therefore follows that the arrow is not moving, since it is in the present. No doubt Zeno's motivation for offering this example of an arrow that does not move was to make it easy to convince people that other things do not move as well.

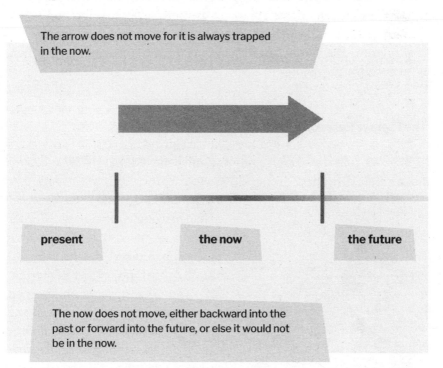

The arrow does not move for it is always trapped in the now.

present

the now

the future

The now does not move, either backward into the past or forward into the future, or else it would not be in the now.

THE RUNNER PARADOX

The most well-known of Zeno's paradoxes is also the simplest. It involves a stationary goal, distance and someone trying to move to the goal. Zeno's thought is that you can never actually get to the goal in this scenario, because you first have to make it to the halfway point between yourself and the goal. But before you make it to that point, you first have to make it to the halfway point between the halfway point and yourself.

And before you make it to the halfway point of the halfway point, you have to make it to the halfway point of the halfway point of the halfway point. As you can imagine, this series of halfway points is endless. In the end, you can never make it because there is an infinite series of halfway points which first have to be achieved. Motion, it turns out, is impossible.

ACHILLES AND THE TORTOISE

Another of these paradoxes is traditionally called Achilles and the Tortoise. In this paradox Achilles is attempting to overtake the tortoise, who has been given a sizable lead since he is so slow. The setup includes the very reasonable assumption that Achilles is faster, much faster than the tortoise. But Achilles never overtakes the tortoise because it is impossible for him to do so. First Achilles must run to the place where the tortoise is at present. The actual distance between them does not matter; there is no need for precision.

The Runner Paradox

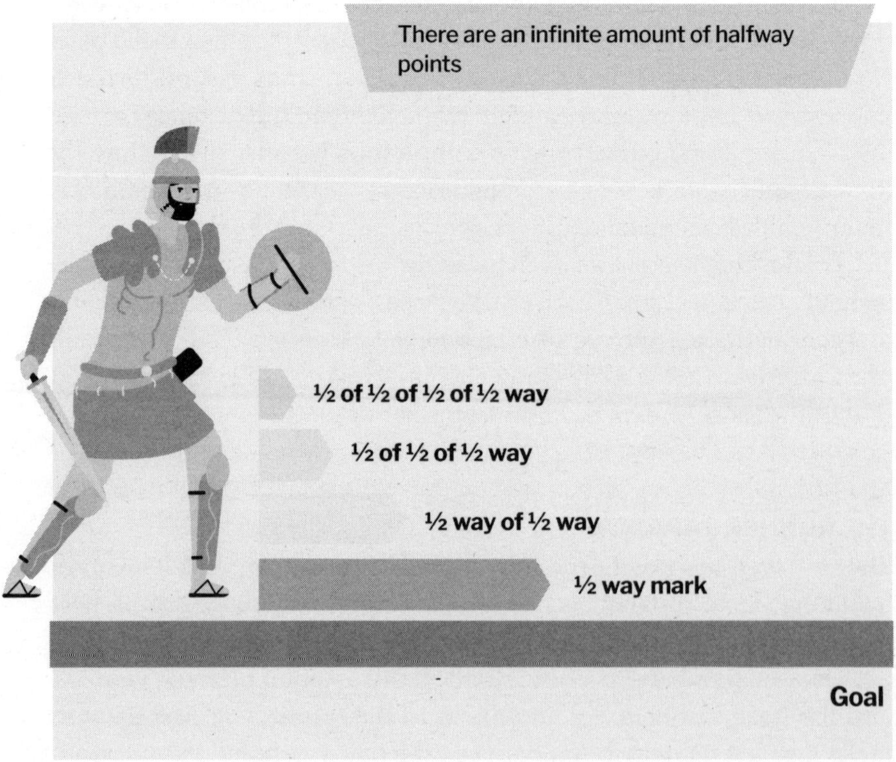

There are an infinite amount of halfway points

½ of ½ of ½ of ½ way

½ of ½ of ½ way

½ way of ½ way

½ way mark

Goal

It is best to conceptualize where Achilles is trying to go to as the *place where the tortoise is* rather than as merely the *tortoise*. For, as we will see in a moment, to try to catch up with the tortoise himself is to get too far ahead of himself (excuse the phrase). It will be enough for Achilles to get himself to the place where the tortoise was when Achilles first set out. If, as Zeno hopes to show, Achilles cannot even get to this place where the tortoise was when he first set out to catch him, then it is all the more certain that he will never overtake and actually catch the tortoise.

The reason that Achilles can never overtake the tortoise is that the tortoise is always on the move. As Achilles sets out, the tortoise moves to a new spot. In fact, because the initial distance between Achilles and the tortoise is sizable, at least in relation to the distance the tortoise can easily manage at whatever pace he takes, Achilles can never catch him. Because in the very process of Achilles moving, the tortoise is moving to a new spot. Now, even though the tortoise is slow, he can more quickly traverse some distance, any distance, than Achilles can make up the distance between himself and the tortoise. To breathe some life into the example, let's just say that the tortoise moves ¼ inch more quickly than Achilles can run ¼ mile, the distance between the two. This seems like a reasonable assumption. So as Achilles attempts to get to the place where the tortoise was at, the tortoise has already moved some distance, more modest and so more quickly managed than the distance covered by Achilles. In fact, this process compounds because every time the tortoise makes some progress, any progress, he can do so more quickly than Achilles can make up the larger distance between the two.

On this characterization of Achilles and the tortoise, Achilles can never actually catch up with the tortoise because there will be an interminable number of these "catch-ups" which have to be completed. Every time the tortoise moves at all, his movements outpace Achilles, not in speed, but in the sense of expanding the number of places where he was and to which Achilles now has to run. The places where Achilles has to run interminably pile up, so he can never actually reach the tortoise.

Zeno's paradoxes appeal to both our experience and our reflection on that experience. Perhaps because of this, they seem to us both possible and impossible, and if they do not convince us that motion is impossible, they force us to wonder how it is possible.

4
Reality as One or Many

Perhaps the most basic philosophical question is whether there is a reality and what it is like. Questions about God's existence or our own place in the universe can in fact be construed as variations of this question, since information about these would be among the most important types of reality we would like to learn about.

Another approach to the inquiry into reality is one that may never have occurred to you. This is the question about whether the universe, taken as everything that exists, is one thing or many. There is an obvious and perhaps trivial sense in which the universe is one in that we designate the totality of what exists by the term "universe." But the Ancient Greeks were fascinated by the question of oneness and multiplicity, a dispute which affected the history of philosophy for a long time to come.

PARMENIDES AND BEING

The most prominent proponent of monism (oneness) in Greece was the philosopher Parmenides (fl. 475 BCE). His works are mostly lost, but we do have a good portion of his poetical work *On Nature*, in which he articulates his arguments for the singularity of the universe. The poem is somewhat strange to modern sensibilities, for a goddess delivers alternate accounts, one of which is the way of truth. As well as espousing his own views, the poem has traditionally been understood to take aim at other philosophical accounts which claim the world is more than just one thing.

Parmenides was the most influential proponent of monism, the idea that everything is one whole. The debate on whether the universe is one or many raged on for centuries.

Monism—the view that there is one material object, namely the universe—does not have a particularly intuitive appeal. We see things, different things, all around us. We are individuals, and we see bicycles, clouds, stars, oceans, bathtubs, and chairs. How could anyone make sense of the idea that all of this is one, much less string together some thoughts to argue that this is the case?

The first step we should take is to discuss Parmenides's concept of being. Like most people, Parmenides thought that if something exists, it is, it has being. This applies to anything, a dog or a shoe. So far, this is uncontroversial and perhaps even too silly to state. But there is a flip side to being—and that is non-being. By "non-being" Parmenides wishes to designate what does not exist and what does not have being, whatever that happens to be. Yet there is something peculiar that happens as we discuss non-being. We can say that non-being does not exist, it is nothing. The crucial thing to hang on to here is that something that is not, *is*.

WHAT "IS" CANNOT FAIL TO BE, OR ELSE IT IS NOT

So far we can sympathize with Parmenides's concept of being and non-being. The real force of Parmenides's being and non-being is the vehemence with which he holds to these definitions. What is, *is*, and what is not, *is not*. This is not a mere repetition. What Parmenides means by this is that if something is, it cannot fail to be what it is. If it stops being what it is, then it fails at being this *is*—but we have already posited that what is, *is*. To say that what is, *is not*, is hogwash. It would be like saying, by

One or many

It would be absurd to say

yellow *is* black

So it would be absurd to say

non-being *is* something which has being

23

analogy, that what is yellow (all over) is black. Except that in the case of being it is even more absurd since yellow and black are not opposites, whereas being and not-being are strict opposites.

More recent analysis of Parmenides's philosophy has shifted focus to the linguistic claim he makes. One of Parmenides's more bold statements of his thesis is that "neither can you know what is not ... nor can you say it." Often the second half has been interpreted to mean that because something does not exist, we cannot talk (or perhaps should refrain from speaking) about what does not exist. A more intriguing possibility arises if we focus at a basic level on what speaking amounts to. One of the assumptions of language is that when we use a word, especially a noun, it refers to something outside ourselves. We are speaking *of* something, when we speak about apples, or bicycles, or clouds. So if we are speaking about something which (we claim) does not exist or has no being, we are actually talking not about non-being but about being. This does not mean that non-being exists, that there is a kind of being for non-being. Rather it means that it is impossible for us to speak about non-being because in the very process of using language, we are unknowingly committing to the idea that what we mention exists, even if in some limited way.

If this interpretation is right, then Parmenides is apparently taking *is* as a synonym for *exists*. Parmenides was undoubtedly interested in the idea of existence. Existence, on his understanding, is capable of being interpreted in at least two ways. The first is the possibility of existence while the other is conceivability. Parmenides views these aspects of existence as closely associated. If something can be conceived of as existing, then it does in fact exist. If it cannot be conceived, then it does not exist.

Parmenides drives home some of his points with a degree of success. One is the idea that if something exists it is possible to think about it. This seems reasonable enough. But more problematic is the idea that what does not exist cannot exist. This is a reformulation of his statement

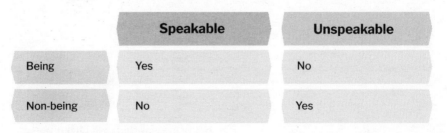

	Speakable	**Unspeakable**
Being	Yes	No
Non-being	No	Yes

that what is not, cannot even be said. It rules out any kind of change or coming into being: birth, creation, ageing, or anything of the sort. Of course, since Parmenides thinks only one thing exists, this is not a problem for him. But if we express Parmenides's thought more clearly, what we are saying is that if something does not exist right now it is impossible for it to exist in the future.

5

The Role of Pleasure in Human Life

Epicurus (341–270 BCE) is most famous as the philosophical founder of Epicureanism, with a reputation, justified or not, as an indulgent and profligate man. The root of this reputation owes to the fact that he was a self-confessed hedonist, one who seeks pleasure, from the Greek word for pleasure, *hedone*.

However, this does not mean that hedonism is somehow an uninformed perspective lacking any reasoned articulation of why it is held or how it is lived.

THE NATURAL SCOPE OF PLEASURE

Epicurus's theory of pleasure arises from his view of the world as essentially physical. Matter is all there is—and of special note, there is no afterlife nor do the gods care for how we act in this life, as they are in a state of distant happiness indifferent to our concerns. Bodily sensation rooted in the physical world was so fundamental to his experience that he said he would not know what pleasures were if it were not for the pleasures of the body. Along with this conceptual formation, there are multiple other ways for Epicurus in which pleasure is primary. Pleasure is what the smallest infant as well as the offspring of animals first seek in life. They seek the pleasure of food, drink, shelter, and companionship. The shared feature between these things is that they conform to the general category of pleasure.

Yet Epicurus did not advocate for an extravagant life of partying and drinking. On the contrary, he thought that the simplest pleasures were the best, such as bread and water. Part of this was prudential: for example, drinking might lead to a hangover, and the overall poor feeling of the hangover has to be calculated into the decision to drink at all. However, there is a positive benefit in living a type of abstemious life. If you eat only bread, and are accustomed to eating bread, you will not only come to enjoy the pleasure of limiting your appetite but will take all the more pleasure on the rare occasion when you are able to partake of fine dining or more food.

KINETIC AND STATIC PLEASURES

We can use this example of the pleasure from taking bread and water compared to dining on caviar and wine as illustrations for the two schemes Epicurus had for the identification of pleasure. In the first scheme Epicurus makes a division between pleasures that are kinetic and pleasures that are static (in technical language, katastematic). The difference is not as clear as it should be, mostly owing to a loss of the texts in which Epicurus discussed these concepts. But the basis of the distinction is that a static pleasure comes about through the restoration or

Epicurus is best known for his belief that we should seek happiness and pleasure above all else—but he viewed avoiding pain as equally important.

replenishment of a natural state, whereas a kinetic pleasure is a pleasure that goes beyond this simple satisfaction. Slaking thirst is an example of a static pleasure, for it restores us to the state in which we do not feel the pain of thirst. The exhilaration of riding a horse at the gallop on a beach is a kinetic pleasure. This kind of pleasure is something over and above the simple satisfaction and restoration of a static pleasure. This does not mean a kinetic pleasure is preferable to a static pleasure; as we will see, what we should aim for is a kind of static pleasure in life.

THE NATURE AND NECESSITY OF PLEASURE

The other scheme or classification of pleasure is threefold. This organization follows from a consideration of whether a pleasure is natural and necessary. So there are pleasures which are *natural and necessary*, to which food, drink, and shelter belong. There are also *natural but unnecessary* pleasures, such as for fancy food and sex. Lastly, *unnatural and unnecessary* pleasures

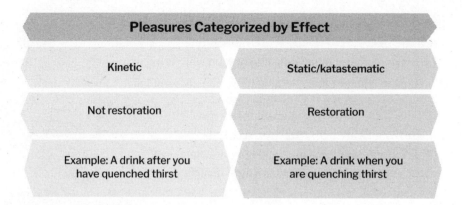

Pleasures Categorized by Effect	
Kinetic	Static/katastematic
Not restoration	Restoration
Example: A drink after you have quenched thirst	Example: A drink when you are quenching thirst

focus on things like power, fame, and wealth. These three pleasures are formed into a hierarchy, with natural and necessary pleasures being what we ought to seek for the most part; natural and unnecessary, what is permissible on occasion; and unnatural and unnecessary, what should be entirely shunned. One possibility that does not show up, which we might expect, is the *unnatural but necessary* pleasure. The reason for this absence is Epicurus's belief that nature provides for us those things she causes us to naturally desire. So if something is going to be necessary for us, like food, it will also be natural. Nature in this providential role will, Epicurus thinks, make what is an object of necessary and natural pleasure like food easy to come by. The necessary pleasure of something like bread is easily available, whereas nature gives no indication it will supply us with a three-course seafood dinner as readily.

Nature provides for us the objects of pleasure such as food and drink, understood as a static pleasure of restoration on one hand and as necessary and natural in another framework. These complementary categorizations of pleasure also bring in another factor central to Epicurus's notion of pleasure: pain. The pleasure of food is a counterpoint to the pain of hunger. We could equally say that the pleasure of food is necessary, for without it the pain of hunger would eventually elevate to the point of death.

Pain plays a central role in hedonism. It is perhaps by contrast with pain that we come to recognize and appreciate pleasure, and it is often pain that precedes pleasure, and pleasure pain. Perhaps the most surprising aspect of pain in Epicurus's system is that he thinks the highest pleasure is nothing but the absence of pain. Any pleasure that is not this absence of pain is simply a variation in the kind of pleasure. That is, the absence of pain is the highest form of pleasure in terms of quality, whereas other pleasures are simply variations that cannot exceed this most desirable state. The recognition that the absence of pain is the highest pleasure also leads Epicurus to identify this absence as the chief good of life. To be without pain in the body and disturbance in the soul is the goal of life.

	Natural	Unnatural
Necessary	Easy to come by, should be sought. Examples: food, drink, shelter	Does not exist. Everything necessary is provided by nature
Unnecessary	Not easy to procure, permissible. Examples: fancy food, sex	Not easy to come by, should be avoided. Examples: money, power, fame

6

Protagoras's "Man is the Measure"

"Man is the measure of all things." Doubtless you have heard this, either in English or its Latin formulation, *homo mensura*. Commonly invoked as the masthead for all humanist endeavor, this phrase goes much further back than the Enlightenment or Renaissance.

The thought, situated in its Greek context, does not have entirely positive connotations. It has been associated with both a denial of truth and a denial that the gods have a say in what is right or best.

"MAN IS THE MEASURE"

The full thought expressed by Protagoras (490–420 BCE) is:

> *"Man is the measure of all things. Of those that are, that they are; and of those that are not, that they are not."*

From the outset, there is a difficulty in determining the scope of Protagoras's statement. Is "man" intended to refer to all men as a collective, the enterprise of humanity, or does it mean each individual man?

An important source for analyzing the meaning of the measure thesis is Plato (428–348 BCE). He interpreted Protagoras to be claiming that as a thing appears to a person, so it is. If while eating chocolate, chocolate appears pleasing to me, then it is pleasing to me. If chocolate appears grotesque to Dorothy, then it is grotesque to Dorothy. In a general sense, this is an identification of the measure thesis with perception. If something is perceived as being a certain way, then it is that way for that person. Perhaps the taste example is too obvious, for we are already prone to concede that taste is a "matter of taste," and we are content to allow each person his or her preference. A less common example that Plato uses is wind. Suppose I have just run a marathon in the sun and now stop in the park. A wind comes and refreshes me in my exhaustion, and I think, "What a nice, cool breeze." By contrast, you have just popped out of your house, which had the air conditioner running. As you come out, you say, "What a hot breeze." The wind is cool to me, and hot to you. How could you possibly convince me or I you that the wind is the opposite of how it feels?

PLATO'S OPPOSITION TO PROTAGORAS

For Plato the consequences of this belief are destructive of truth and so dangerous. For if we cannot perceive how things really are, then we cannot get at the truth. Food and wind and our reactions to them are quite trivial. But what about things such as beauty and justice? The idea that beauty or justice is one thing for one person and an entirely different thing for someone else was an unacceptable conclusion for Plato. Plato rejected the implications of the measure thesis, but it is likely that Protagoras meant something much broader than merely perception. He probably

What is the wind *really*, hot or cold?

Wind

Feels hot to Jack

Feels cold to Jill

intended that "man is the measure" was applicable to judgments of all kinds, not merely those acquired by our sense perceptions.

If we express the measure thesis broadly, we might do well to construe it under the concept of *relativism*. The most forceful formulation of this idea is that any belief is as good as any other on any topic whatsoever. It is important to point out that in discussing the measure thesis in this way, we are firmly in the domain of knowing and knowledge. This is not a legal claim, that people do or should have the right to think or believe what they want.

THE INCONSISTENCY OF THE MEASURE THESIS

If any two opinions are equally good, what exactly does this mean? Plato, for instance, thought that this view was inconsistent and impossible. Imagine two people had two different and incompatible beliefs. You say, "Picasso's art is great," and your friend says, "Picasso art is wretched." You then say, cleverly, "I believe your opinion on Picasso is wrong." Your friend, the Picasso hater, adhering to the measure thesis, must admit that to you it is correct that her own opinion is wrong. Thus Picasso's art actually is great. The spirit of relativism leaves itself open to self-refutation. The idea can even be applied more directly to the measure thesis itself: I disagree with the measure thesis, so that it is true to me that "man is the measure" is in fact false. The consequence is that man is not the measure.

There is a clear sense in which the measure thesis, or at least a subdued version, is true. This is the claim that things do not appear the same to everyone in the same way. Sometimes differences in perception are great: I think this is a shade of green, while you think it is blue. Sometimes our perceptions radically differ: I think this is good, you think it is bad. There is an acknowledgement that we cannot help but think and perceive how we do think and perceive, and this is a function of who we are. Two consequences seem to follow from this. The first is that we cannot escape from interpreting the world from our perspective. The second, a serious threat to the practice of philosophy, is that because we have beliefs about the world being a certain way, formed from our perspective, we cannot persuade each other without a fundamental change in outlook.

One way to avoid this bleak conclusion—that truth about the world is forever foreclosed from us because we each are wearing our own "spectacles"—is to acknowledge a gap between what is believed and what is true. "It appears to me to be this way" communicates something about myself and my relation to the world. Strictly speaking, however, it does not weigh in on the nature of what is and is not true. It is in this way that the doctrine of *homo mensura* can be rescued from the possibility of slipping into solipsism, the belief that only the self (and no one else) exists. "Man is the measure" is more about the person measuring than what is measured.

Everything is relative refutes itself

7

The Sorites Paradox

Sorites (so-RYE-tees) is the Ancient Greek word for a heap of sand. The sorites paradox arises from a simple feature of a heap. Although the idea behind the paradox is straightforward, any resolution of its tension requires untangling several difficulties.

So perplexing is it that the ancient school of Skeptics capitalized on the difficulties encountered in the sorites paradox as one of multiple ways to cast doubt on the possibility of knowledge.

INTRODUCING THE PROBLEM OF THE SORITES

A man comes up to you and says he is confused. He wants to know what a heap is, and if you can help him by pointing one out. As you agree, he pulls out a bucket of sand and a pair of tweezers. You watch and he takes one grain of sand and places it on the ground, and asks, "Is this a heap?" You laugh and say no. Then he adds a second grain to the first, and a third to the second, at each stage asking whether he now has a heap before him. You say no to each, but you begin to grow nervous, since you see where this is going. He is going to keep asking after every added grain whether what stands in front of you is in fact a heap. At

Sorites

At what point do we have a heap?

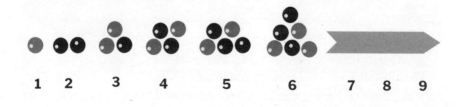

1 2   3   4   5   6   7   8   9

How many hairs can he lose until he becomes "bald"?

what point do you say that it is a heap—at 100, at 101, or 1,000? This is the central issue in the sorites paradox, determining at what stage there is a sorites and at which previous stage there was not.

Now, the sorites paradox need not be limited to heaps. It can also be applied to terms like *bald* or *old*. If a man has 100,000 hairs, we would not say he is bald, but what if he has only 100? At some point a determination must be made. This dynamic nature of the paradox led to a cottage industry in antiquity of fabricating ever more examples.

There are still more issues connected to the sorites. As well as adding grain by grain, we can subtract grain from grain, and go backward from a heap that already exists. At each step, again, we can ask when it ceases being a heap. We are similarly perplexed in the backward case as in the forward about determining when a group of sand is or is not a heap.

THE STEPWISE PERPLEXITY OF THE SORITES

Another puzzling aspect of the paradox is the way in which the logic of the sorites works. It is agreed, of course, that one grain of sand does not constitute a heap. But if at any given stage, you say, "Now it is a heap," something very strange happens. Suppose the 500-grain mark is when you say you now have the heap, meaning that at 499 there is no heap. What you have just admitted is that adding one grain makes a heap. But back when you started counting the heaps, you agreed that one grain was not a heap, so it is odd that now one grain makes the difference between something being or not being a heap. This can be put in a different way which appeals more to our common sense: we find it hard to believe that taking away a single grain of sand will cause a heap to no longer be a heap, since whatever a heap is, it is large enough to admit of missing a single grain of sand.

One grain, it can be argued in a different way, is an almost immeasurable and insubstantial amount compared to a heap. So if we start with a heap, then of course taking a single grain away does nothing. But this admission

If you can always take one grain away and have a heap, then this leads to one grain being a heap.

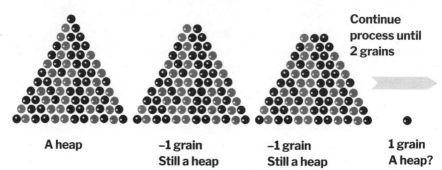

Continue process until 2 grains

| A heap | −1 grain Still a heap | −1 grain Still a heap | 1 grain A heap? |

can be used to the consenter's disadvantage, leading to the conclusion that even a single grain is a heap. If we say that 1,000 grains is a heap, then taking one grain leaves us with 999 grains and this is a heap. If we have 999 grains and take one grain, we have 998 grains and this is a heap. We can continue this process and at every stage, all the way down to a single grain, we can say that there is a heap. We can say this because a heap is something that still remains a heap if you take one grain away. This seems hard to deny, since the nature of a heap of things is to be able to endure the slightest possible diminution, the quantity of a grain.

The sorites paradox, as we see it so far, brings up issues of ambiguity, precision, definition, language, and even the possibility of mathematics. There is also something to be observed in the very process of the paradox. At no point is there a direct comparison of a single grain to a heap; rather the paradox arises gradually, as we proceed from one stage to the next.

WHAT IS THE PROBLEM WITH SORITES?

The vagueness of terms used in sorites, such as *heap, bald,* or *old,* has led some philosophers to abandon the concept behind the paradox. This is a drastic step, for it effectively denies that there is such a term as *heap,* or that it can be employed meaningfully in everyday language. Another equally dramatic move is to "bite the bullet"—not concerning the fact that there is no such thing as a heap, but by doggedly affirming that there are heaps and they are defined by a certain number. So a heap just is 500 grains, and 499 is not. The justification for this need only consist in the convention of language. Our saying so ratifies the truthfulness of a heap being 500 grains of sand.

One last method for solving the sorites paradox involves a distinction between language and knowing. That is, a *heap* is a vague term which can be applied with some freedom without any commitment as to our knowledge. It may or may not be a heap, whatever that could mean, but the term is employed for the very fact that it is vague.

8

The Skeptical Outlook

Skeptic is a word thrown around with some regularity in the modern world, connoting a somewhat adversarial attitude coming from a position of doubt. This is not wholly off the mark for how skepticism worked in the ancient world. However, skepticism as a philosophical movement was sophisticated and principled. An entire movement in itself, it manifested in two major schools.

THE ACADEMIC SKEPTICS

Academic skepticism, named for its genesis in Plato's Academy, did not originate at the time of Plato but much later after his death, through an analysis of his texts. Socrates, in Plato's dialogues, famously inquired after the definitions of such abstractions as courage or temperance. There was often no definite conclusion at the end of these dialogues, and this feature of Platonic texts, combined with Socrates's profession of ignorance, led to the adoption of skepticism in the Academy.

After Plato's death, a singular philosopher would attain the seat of Plato as the leader of the Academy, until he in turn was replaced at death by yet another. One such leader was Arcesilaus (c. 316–241 BCE), who introduced skepticism into the Academy around the time he took it over, from c. 268 to 266 BCE. He conducted philosophy in an oral manner, leaving no written work. This manifested in a method of dialectic exchange, or discussion, in which the views of another were subjected to investigation. This investigation was performed not just to find out what the interlocutor believed, but rather to test what was being said—and to do so in the light of other beliefs held by the interlocutor rather than some standard held out by the skeptics as the truth. By following this procedure, the skeptics were able to root out inconsistencies in the many beliefs of their contemporaries.

A Roman depiction of Plato's Academy. At some point after Plato's death, his Academy began to cultivate the skeptical philosophical doctrine.

If this description sounds adversarial, there is good reason. The skeptics were involved in a bitter philosophical dispute with the Stoic school at this time. In particular, almost as if designed to flout aggressive skeptical attacks on belief, the Stoics posited that there was a *criterion of truth*.

A STANDARD FOR ACQUIRING THE TRUTH

The criterion of truth is a certain type of impression made on our minds from viewing the outside world. The term *impression* was originally a metaphor conveying the idea that truth presses itself into the mind like a mold pressing into hot wax. On the force of this metaphor the Stoics termed this process of apprehending the truth a *cognitive impression*. A

Would you be able to tell apart:

A wax apple *from* **a real apple?**

One egg *from* **another?**

cognitive impression reveals some aspect of the world as it really is, and for this reason is true. The specifics of how, and even if, this criterion of truth was conceived of as resulting in truth has been a point of dispute up to the present day. In general terms, what the criterion of truth purported to establish was that we can have a perception of some aspect of the world which is wholly faithful and true to how the world actually is. It is best to think of the criterion of truth as both a thing and a method. It is a thing in that it is something which is true, and it is a method in the way that these cognitive impressions manifest themselves to us. At any rate, a cognitive impression has a special nature which, so to speak, announces itself as true. When we experience this announcement of truth, and only when we experience it, we are supposed to consent to the impression—and it is at this point that one has a hold of truth.

Needless to say, Academic skeptics were not satisfied with the Stoic criterion. The main thrust of their skeptical objection was that there could be, and in fact are, impressions which are false and are indistinguishable from these cognitive impressions. One of the more famous examples is an apple sitting next to its wax likeness. You could look at the two sitting on the table together and you could just as easily grab the wax version and mistakenly take a bite out of it.

PYRRHONIAN SKEPTICISM

A more radical form of skepticism arises in the figure of Pyrrho (360–270 BCE), whose works are lost but whose views are partially preserved and reformulated by later philosophers in his tradition. If we trace the development of skepticism from the Academy to its Pyrrhonian variety, doubt was now being applied to all beliefs and appearances. In this reinforced system of skepticism, skepticism itself was elevated to a way of life. The goal of skepticism was to achieve tranquility of the mind.

Tranquility is achieved in several ways. First it should be understood that beliefs are the sources which disrupt or altogether eliminate this tranquility. The most obvious example is the great variety of beliefs exposed by other philosophical schools advocating this or that doctrine, positions which often turn out to be refuted by other philosophers. Besides, the activity of disputing, prompted by commitment to these dogmas, results in a disturbance of the tranquility of mind. In addition to these more obvious cases, in which a life of philosophical squabbling leads to a disturbance in tranquility, there is also the concern that beliefs of any kind, no matter how seemingly innocuous, likewise lead to the quenching of our tranquility.

This bust of Pyrrho perhaps reflects an external calm springing from inner tranquility.

BELIEF OPPOSED TO TRANQUILITY

How then does belief lead to a disturbance of the mind? Several things can be said on this account. We often act according to our beliefs, and if our beliefs are wrong, our actions will be different as well. For instance, if we think it is going to rain, we will put on a raincoat and boots and take an umbrella. Even if it doesn't rain, our behavior has still been affected: we have dressed differently. We have no way, according to the skeptic, to determine the truth. If we take tranquility as one of the goals of life, beliefs do nothing but hinder our acquisition of it.

The path to tranquility is blocked by belief, so we must eliminate belief. But how is this done? One overarching tactic appealed to by the Pyrrhonists was an attempt to cancel out belief. If someone believed that

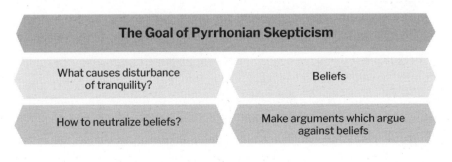

The Goal of Pyrrhonian Skepticism	
What causes disturbance of tranquility?	Beliefs
How to neutralize beliefs?	Make arguments which argue against beliefs

eyes are the faithful reporters of reality, the skeptics made arguments to show how eyes are unreliable. By making strong counterarguments, they could persuade people not that one or the other side was correct, but that both were apparently equally right and so equally wrong. This led to the suspension of belief and to the aim of skeptics: tranquility.

9

Plato's Allegory of the Cave

A cave has many associations, several of which are primal and mysterious. Darkness, fear, secrets, dens of animals, robbers, and exploration can be evoked when we think of a cave. The cave is also the setting of arguably the most famous image in the history of philosophy. The Allegory of the Cave, as it has come to be known, appears in Book VII of Plato's *Republic*.

The allegory is filled with vivid and arresting imagery although it is not itself very complicated. Nevertheless the allegory has several different levels of interpretation.

THE ALLEGORY OF THE CAVE SUMMARIZED

First we need to describe the allegory in the way that the character Socrates explains it in the *Republic*. We are to envision a large cave with prisoners in it. These people have been kept in the cave since childhood and thus have no conception of the outside world. In fact, since they have been shackled by their arms and legs inside the cave for their whole lives, they do not even know there is a world outside the cave.

In the darkness of this cave there is a fire providing some light. But the light of this fire is unusual. The prisoners have their backs to the light so that they cannot see the fire directly but instead are forced to see shadows cast on the cave wall in front of them. Unbeknown to them, a low wall has been built out of sight, behind the prisoners and in front of the fire. Just as a marionette show has a low wall to obscure human hands moving the puppets, this low wall has also been built to hide people behind it. The people who are behind this wall have different objects made of different material, which they are carrying and hold just above the wall. Because these objects are between the fire and the wall,

The Allegory of the Cave: a prisoner sees a strange shadow on the cave wall and perceives this as reality.

they cast a shadow on the wall. The people who carry these strange objects are walking and talking with each other as the prisoners watch the strange shadows move on the wall. The shadows are accompanied by the speech of the object-carriers, since the sound also echoes off the wall into the ears of the prisoners. With this very peculiar scenario in our head, Socrates asks us whether the prisoners will think that the shadows move about on their own and are also the source of the echoes. The answer seems to be a saddening and inevitable yes, given that the prisoners have no experience of anything outside the cave.

The above communicates the poor plight of the prisoners. But Socrates is not done. For after describing this situation, he knows that readers will be eager to set the prisoners free. The question is how this will be achieved. But freedom for the prisoners will not come quickly or easily; it must proceed in steps. To begin with, prisoners set free from their shackles will be very weak from having sat in an emaciated condition their whole lives. When they are helped up and turn towards the fire, they will be blinded by its brilliance, since they have seen only the dimmed flickering flames on the wall.

A PARTIAL EXPLANATION OF THE ALLEGORY

At this point in the story, Socrates starts to give a partial analysis. Since a freed prisoner can only stand and look at the fire in pain, and is accustomed to living a life of looking at the dim light of shadows, he will prefer his old life. Even if you show him the objects that were being carried about, and demonstrate how he is one step closer to seeing reality as it actually is, he would prefer his old way of life being shackled up.

If the prisoner who has been freed from this oppression rejects his freedom upon being shown the fire and the objects behind the shadows, it is all the more true that he will go kicking and screaming if someone drags him to the surface where the sun actually shines. This transition

The freed prisoners will try to save others, but will be killed.

will bring great pain and anger. To become used to the sun, the prisoner will have to look only at shadows at first, and then at the images of people and objects reflected in water and mirrors. After this period, he will finally be able to acknowledge and appreciate the truth. Now freed, the prisoner will want to go back into the cave to free others. However, when he returns to the cave his eyes will be ill-adjusted to the darkness. The other prisoners whom he is trying to free will note his difficulty in adjusting to the world of the cave which they know, and will dismiss his efforts to convince them to leave, on the grounds that this will only hurt their own eyes as well. In the end the prisoners will not only reject the savior, but kill him.

THE GENERAL PICTURE THE CAVE ILLUSTRATES

The Allegory of the Cave powerfully illustrates many of the metaphysical themes in the preceding books of the *Republic*. Although the allegory undoubtedly contains political commentary and elements—especially at the end, where Plato the author gives a not-so-subtle hint that Athens killed Socrates for trying to enlighten people about the nature of truth— the purpose of the illustrations is to tell us about the nature of reality.

We are ignorant of the true nature of reality according to Plato, in which there is the sensible world of physical things and appearances as well as the "real" world of the intelligibles. In the allegory, the outside world of the sun is the intelligible world, while the inner world of the cave is our sensible world. The visible and sensible worlds are themselves divided into two. The invisible world is divided into reason, which contains Plato's Forms, and intellect which has numbers and shapes. The sensible world contains physical objects and images. In the allegory physical objects are represented by the objects before the fire while images are the shadows.

Plato's Allegory of the Cave sets forth a world in which there is a hierarchy of existence, showing that we must not only ascend to the highest level of reason, but that our journey will be difficult and lonely. To escape the cave is to be by oneself.

10
Plato's Forms

Few ideas in philosophy are as often referred to and equally as misunderstood as Plato's theory of Forms. Someone will have a good meal and exclaim, "That was the Platonic Form of food." This and similar uses of the term Platonic Form do convey something of what Plato had in mind, but mostly miss the mark.

The doctrine of Forms is sophisticated, with several distinct features, and there is even something mysterious, if not downright mystical, about it.

THE ORIGIN OF FORMS

How and why Plato developed the doctrine is disputed, but one key motivation is that he was keen to preserve the possibility of truth and knowledge. He felt that the world we see around us is fleeting and ever changing. This mutable nature of the world indicates a need to shift to more solid ground, to find that which does not or, even better, cannot change. Plato's solution was a world beyond matter and all the senses, a realm of which our world is a dim reflection and imitation. There is the world as we see it, and a greater world beyond our senses. This distinction between the two worlds not only captures the superior nature of the world beyond, but also secures the possibility of knowledge. For Plato, if something is changing, it cannot be known. The simplest way to articulate this strange belief is to say that it is hard, if not impossible, to say and to know that something is the same thing after changing.

THE FORMS ARE IMMATERIAL

The easiest path to understanding what the Forms are is by understanding what they are not, by contrasting them with our everyday world. The world has many objects in it. As an example, let us assume that there are such things as beautiful trees. Any single one of these trees we can call a *particular*. This is for the simple reason that each tree is an individual thing. The world

Plato thought that some permanent entities must exist to explain how individual things exist and how we come to know this.

is full of these particulars: flowers, people, houses. But we can also call these individuals "particulars" in contrast to the Forms. This is because the Forms are absolutely unique. Forms are one of a kind, and it is in virtue of the fact that Forms exist that particulars are also able to exist. We will return to this idea in a moment, but for now it suffices to say that, in the context of speaking about beautiful trees, which are many, there is but a single Form of Beauty and a single Form of Tree.

This description of the Forms sounds strange, for the idea thus far may conjure up the idea of a tree, or whatever Form is under consideration, sitting enthroned somewhere. But Plato conceived of the Forms as not existing in a physical place at all. This accounted for their immateriality, and imperceptibility, as well as their eternality and divinity. The Forms are themselves unchangeable, in contrast to particulars which are highly mutable, material and perceptible, mortal, and temporary, in general opposite to the Forms.

PARTICIPATION IN FORMS

If Forms and particulars are in this fundamental sense opposed to each other, how do they share anything in common? Sticking to the example above, how can there be a Form of Beauty and a particular that is beautiful? Plato believed that a particular *participates* in a Form. He was notoriously unclear about the details of this relationship. Overall, the concept of participation communicates the superiority of the Form and the dependence of the particular on the Form. Every particular in our world depends on a Form for its existence and nature. The beautiful tree participates in the Form of Tree as well as the Form of Beauty. The Form is said to serve as a model for the particular. But the notion of participation is more rigorous than mere resemblance: the particular partakes of the Form but is limited by its finiteness from being more than a particular, from being a Form.

FORMS AS MODELS OR PARADIGMS

So the Forms are exemplars or models for particulars, but why? For one, Plato thought that Forms were needed to explain the consistency that different particulars shared. For instance, if a woman, a car, and a painting are all "beautiful," how can this be the case if they are all so different? Likewise, if a woman who is beautiful ages, how can it come about that she who *is* beautiful will no longer be beautiful? By having many beautiful things *participate* in the Form of Beauty, Plato overcame this difficulty: the Form itself was what was beautiful, and all beautiful things are only beautiful insofar as they participate or share in the Form of Beauty.

The above description can be applied generally, so that we can say that if something "is X," as in "Socrates is just," "the bed is large," "the marriage is good," they are X by participating in the Form of X. So the just man Socrates participates in the Form of the Just or Justice. If he ever becomes unjust, it is because he stops participating in the Form of the Just. For Plato the Forms are the source of X, and this not only means that particulars must borrow their X-ness from the Form, but it entails that the Forms have a perfect and unchangeable relationship to X. If we are to say it most properly, the Forms do not so much possess X as they are X. The Form of Beauty is beautiful not because it possesses beauty but because the Form of Beauty is beauty.

Plato's "Two Worlds"	
Our World	**A World Beyond**
Full of particles	Where Forms exist
Changing	Unchanging
Mortal	Immortal
Not divine	Divine
Material	Immaterial
Perceptible	Imperceptible

THE GENERAL IMPORTANCE OF FORMS

If all this were not enough, Plato also believes that Forms give a solid foundation for morality and linguistic expressions, since they do not change and allow us to refer and compare our behavior or language to something which does not change. The unchanging nature of the Forms is ultimately simple. They explain and account for the being of all the physical world. In some dialogues, however, Plato was hesitant to have Forms for everything, such as for mud or hair—indicating that even for him, Forms have some limitations.

Particular trees

The Form of Tree

The Form of Tree

Particular tree

Trees participate in
the Form of Tree

We are able to grasp the idea
of a tree by the Form of a tree

Idea of a tree

Form

11

Epicurus's Swerve

The atomic nature of matter, and ourselves, is a given in the modern imagination. Yet this idea is not scientific if we are to be true to history. Rather, it first appeared as a philosophical idea promoted by the Greek philosopher Democritus (460–370 BCE), then was adapted by Epicurus (341–270 BCE) and explained by one of Epicurus's later Roman adherents, Lucretius (99–55 BCE).

As is the case with any philosophical idea, there are also problems which arise with this version of atomism. One of the tensions was between free will and atoms. If everything is just atoms, as Democritus believed, then our actions and even the beliefs behind our actions are nothing more than atoms. If this is true, then what atoms are and how they behave, not what we do and think, will determine our behavior and thoughts. This is a real problem, and Epicurus had to introduce some feature into his atomic theory in order to solve it. His solution is one of the most famous and infamous ideas in ancient philosophy: the swerve.

EPICURUS'S UNIVERSE

Before we look at the swerve, we first need to establish the context in which the swerve was operating, the physical universe. For Epicurus, there are two things in the universe: the atoms and the void. The universe, made up of these two aspects, is itself infinite. The atoms are of course situated *in* the void, and the void, being nothing at all, proves to be no source of support or foundation for the atoms. So the result of this setup is that the atoms are perpetually falling in the void. The void, since it is nothing and has no properties, can offer no resistance at all to the atoms falling in it. Lacking any resistance to their fall, the atoms gather an incredible speed as they pass through the void. What accounts for the speed of the atoms is their weight, which also determines their direction downward, ever downward, unless there is some collision or there is a congregation of atoms into something larger.

THE NATURE OF ATOMS

Just as with the modern notion of atoms, the atoms of Epicurus are microscopic and so their true nature is hidden from our observation. Even though there is a finite set of different kinds of atoms, the atoms as a whole are infinite in number. We are ourselves part of the atoms falling in the void despite the appearance of being stationary. Occasionally the atoms gather into shapes which we come to view as humans, animals, or trees. The different shapes of the atoms account for the differing qualities or properties of things. For example, the atoms of gold are hard and shiny, while those of the soul are the finest and spherical, allowing our thought to move very quickly.

If it seems impossible that our own bodies are an accumulation of atoms falling in the void, Lucretius offers us the analogy of a flock of sheep moving on a distant mountain. From afar, the flock seems like a stationary white splotch on the side of the mountain; it is only when we get closer that we realize that this white circle is moving and is composed of individual sheep, like atoms. This is the way that Lucretius argues,

The scientific concept of an "atom" ultimately derives from Democritus's philosophical notion of something "uncuttable," which is unable to be reduced to anything smaller.

on behalf of Epicurus, that all atoms, even those which are a part of apparently solid unified objects, are falling in the void.

THE IDEA OF THE ATOMIC SWERVE

It is at this point that we can introduce the swerve. Since all the atoms are falling parallel to each other in a straight line due to their own weight, how do they come to be organized into things as we know them, such as animals and plants? The answer to this question is the first reason Lucretius gives as he introduces the swerve. The swerve is a completely random and unpredictable movement in the falling of these atoms. It is meant to explain the creation of natural objects. On Lucretius's telling, the atoms are combined and arranged by the "blows" of atoms hitting each other from this random swerve. Everything is falling in parallel until unexpectedly a single atom deviates from its course, striking a blow on another atom, in turn causing a chain reaction which results in the creation of a tree or a bird. This swerve deviates from a line imperceptibly, making only the smallest movement away from straightness, as Lucretius thinks it would be hard to believe that atoms moving rectilinearly due to their own weight could shoot out at a perpendicular angle. Without a swerve,

The Universe

Infinite void   +   Infinite atoms

The atoms are eternally falling downward through the void

nature, the personified creative force, is unable to create anything, as all atoms would continue on as before, falling in an unbroken straight line.

But there is more to the swerve than how atoms come together to form the familiar objects of our world. The swerve is also meant to counteract the view that atoms falling in the void makes free will impossible. For if atoms are always falling in the same way, and everything that exists is made of atoms, then atoms completely determine how things are. But if there is a swerve in atoms, unpredictable in cause and occasion, this makes room for free will. Lucretius thinks that this swerve can account for free will and explains our choices.

THE SWERVE ACCOUNTS FOR FREE WILL

The way that Lucretius has the swerve account for the possibility of free will is quite interesting. The swerve serves as a contrast to the material makeup of the body, which is made up only of atoms. He thinks that the way atoms influence atoms is easily distinguished from how minds influence atoms, and this proves that the mind is free from atomic influence. He asks us to imagine a horse standing at a starting gate and the moment when the gate is opened. Even though the horse tells its body to move at that exact moment, it takes some fraction of time for this to happen. By contrast, when a body acts on a body—that is, atom on atom—the reaction is immediate, such as a hammer striking a nail. So our mind works in a way independent of the atom and the void, while indicating that there are other things in the universe: free will and the swerve.

The swerve: a slight random deviation of the downward motion of an atom

swerving atom

collision of atom results in natural objects like a tree or animal

12

Epicurus on the Fear of Death

Today Epicurus (341–270 BCE), when thought of at all, is often only conjured up by the word *Epicurean*, someone given to pleasure. While he was indeed a philosopher of pleasure, this commitment also included the shunning of pain or fear. In his mind, the chief fear of every human is the fear of death. There are two aspects to this fear.

One is the traditional association of death with a judgment in the afterlife. The other is death itself, considered as the moment of expiration and the state we find ourselves in at death. The truth, according to Epicurus, is that we have nothing to fear, and he offers some compelling reasons to think this is so. He begins with the assumption that the fear of death does not arise from an entirely emotional source, but relies on a set of beliefs about what will harm us when we die. As opposed to the traditional beliefs of his time—that someone who dies will continue to live on after death, perhaps as an immortal soul—Epicurus teaches that the end of life is the end of it all. When once you die, there is nothing left of you.

THE DEATH OF THE BODY IS THE END OF US

What pulls Epicurus toward this belief is his commitment to materialism, the idea that matter or physical stuff is all that exists or can exist. On this understanding of the world, the body consists of nothing but matter, so that when the body dies, there is no soul, no further *self*, which can escape the body and continue to exist apart from the body. Thus all thought and perception are extinguished entirely at the moment of death. The upshot of all this is that we need not fear death because we will not be there to experience it as it happens. Epicurus puts it this way: when we are, death is not, and when death is, we are not. This phrasing memorably

Lucretius was a later Roman proponent of Epicurus and Epicureanism.

captures not only the finality and completeness of death, but also emphasizes that upon the approach of death we are no longer there to meet it, for death simply is the loss of the ability to notice or feel or think about anything. Death cannot come for us in this sense, for it is not actually something with its own independent existence. Rather, death is the label for that state when we stop existing.

The association of death with the cessation of our bodily perceptions logically ties into Epicurus's theories about pleasure and pain. Epicurus identifies the purpose of human activity as seeking pleasure and avoiding pain. While this does not exclusively involve the body, the pursuit of pleasure is to a large degree experienced through the body. To be dead is to be incapable of pleasure or pain, but it also means that were we (impossibly) to survive beyond the death of our bodies, this kind of life would not be worth living because it would be void of pleasure.

THE OTHER EVILS SURROUNDING DEATH

Lucretius (99–55 BCE) has many imaginative arguments to eliminate the evil which we perceive death to be or to show it as an outright good. One worry which he faces head-on is the sadness that comes into our minds as we consider the loss of friends and family when we die. This is as much about our death in the future as it is our mourners' well-being. The person who is contemplating his future death should recognize that he will be free from all pains and fears when he is dead, and his family and friends who are mourning should actually rejoice since he is relieved of any possibility of suffering.

DEATH IN THE BANQUET ANALOGY

Lucretius also compares life and death to a banquet to indicate how we should be grateful for life and enjoy it to the full. As we are dining at a fancy banquet, we do not think to ourselves that we eat and drink in vain for soon the party will be over and we will never be able to relive this

The Banquet Analogy to Death

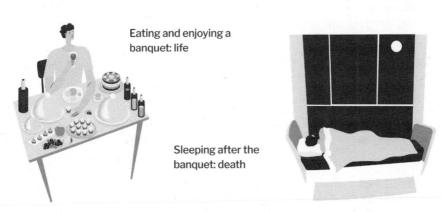

Eating and enjoying a banquet: life

Sleeping after the banquet: death

party again. Rather, we enjoy it just as we should enjoy life. The proper time to enjoy the banquet is at the banquet, and then it is time to return to one's house and go to sleep. And when we fall asleep in our beds after the banquet, we do not sit up and refuse to sleep because the banquet is over, but willingly accept that it is now time to go to sleep, even though sleep will be a time when the memories of the banquet will be absent from us. In the same way, we should willingly and gladly slip into the permanent sleep of death when it is our time to go after a long life.

THE SYMMETRY ARGUMENT: DEATH IS LIKE OUR PRE-EXISTENT STATE

Lucretius was fond of analogies such as the banquet comparison, and he also likened the state of death itself to being the reflection of a mirror. Nature herself is the one holding up the mirror and what it is reflecting is the state before we were born. Before we were born, we did not have any trouble or difficulty in the world, and we did not care about anything since we did not exist. Nor, on the other hand, are we currently distressed about our non-existence before we were born. Since we will be in the same state at death as we were before birth, we should likewise not worry about death just as we do not worry about the time before our birth. In this way there is a symmetry between our pre-existence and our death: neither is bad, and so we should not fear or give thought to death just as in the case of our pre-existence.

Somewhat paradoxically Lucretius's arguments about death can still offer some solace to anyone who believes in an immortal soul but wants to hedge their bets. That is, even if the soul is not immortal and death is indeed the end of us, this will cause us no harm, for we will be absent when death is finally present.

The Symmetry Argument: pre-existence is similar to death

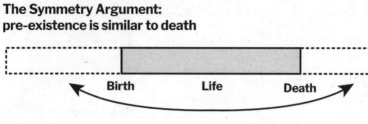

Pre-existence is similar to death

Two states are identical

Post-existence

13

The Four Causes

We know, says Aristotle (384–322 BCE), when we know the causes of things, whether this is a specific or general domain of knowledge. The cause of a thing, in the popular understanding, is what immediately precedes some effect, and a cause is thought to have brought its effect about.

We say the cause of World War II was the invasion of Poland, or that love is the cause of marriage. Things of the first kind cause things of the second kind when they bring them about. Aristotle partly retains this intuitive approach to cause, but his understanding comprehends four different meanings of *cause*.

NATURE AS THE ORIGIN OF CAUSES

To better appreciate the way in which Aristotle understands cause, it is important to first understand the role of nature. This is not only because the concept of an individual nature itself plays a strong role in the causes, but also because the general notion of nature (as in Mother Nature) is in some sense Aristotle's starting point. This means that Aristotle looks to nature as a kind of model in which it is easier to see the four causes at work. Additionally, Aristotle thinks that the four causes as seen in nature are superior to the four causes in human endeavors, which are nothing more than imitations of nature.

Aristotle lists four causes. He never comes out and says so, but by the way he describes them, he seems to think that in every explanation all four causes are present.

THE MATERIAL CAUSE

The easiest cause to understand is the *material cause*. This cause is what something is physically composed of. The material cause of a chair is wood, while that of a shirt is cotton. These are rather simple examples, and in the case of something as complex as a car, the fabric, oil, metal, glass, and so forth, would all together be the material cause.

THE EFFICIENT CAUSE

The *efficient cause* is that which is the first motion bringing something about. This can be understood as motion or change. So the father is the efficient cause of the child. If we consider a horseshoe, the blacksmith is the efficient cause of the shoe. In a more abstract sense, Aristotle would also consider the art of blacksmithing to be the efficient cause of the horseshoe. One reason he might have thought this is that it is the art of blacksmithing residing in and being expressed by the blacksmith which brings the horseshoe into being.

THE FORMAL CAUSE

The *formal cause* is that which a thing is in the sense of a form. The meaning of "form" as used by Aristotle can be taken as synonymous with "definition." We will see why after we have looked at the idea of form. It is easier to see what this means in simple cases and from there to extend the concept to more sophisticated instances. Take a simple fork. What is the formal cause? Its material cause is a metal of some kind, and the efficient cause is the producer of the silverware. The formal cause is the shape of the fork. The shape of a fork is a metal object with an elongated handle terminating in four prongs. Notice that in describing the shape of the fork we have also offered a definition of the fork. The definition of a fork is in one way nothing other than a description of the fork. This convenient coincidence of the definition and the shape of something does not always come together so clearly, if at all. But this fork example nicely demonstrates that the core meaning for Aristotle of a formal cause is its *form*, where the form is a synonym for shape, and the shape itself of the thing conveys and expresses the definition. Now the form and the definition are not always so pat. The shape and definition of a submarine and a tree do not converge with such neatness. For the mere shape alone of a tree would not only leave out the biological functions and its sophisticated internal operations, but could not even reflect that it is a living thing. A fake non-living tree—for instance, a plastic Christmas tree—would be the same shape as a living tree.

What are the causes of a fork?

THE FINAL CAUSE

The *final cause* is simultaneously both the most abstract and most understandable of the causes. Often when we know what something is *for*, we have the best understanding of what it is. If you are presented with some strange mechanical device, whose appearance does not immediately announce its function or use, you would naturally ask, "What is it for?" If told "It's for catching mice," or "It's for cracking nuts," you think you have a grasp on its true essence.

In his discussion of the final cause, Aristotle does not in fact use the term final. Instead he describes it as the *"for the sake of which."* One exercises for the sake of health and a nation goes to war for the sake of victory, where health and victory are the final causes. This sheds light on a slightly different emphasis which Aristotle sometimes gives to the final cause—the beneficiary or the person for whom something is done. You can write a poem to impress a love interest. In this case the *"for the sake of which"* and the beneficiary are the same—the love interest.

The Four Causes

1) Material cause of a chair: wood

2) Efficient cause of a chair: carpenter

The four causes are linked together by the final cause. The final cause, the purpose of the whole, determines both the material and the efficient causes, while the material and efficient causes work together to bring about the formal cause. For instance, suppose there is a carpenter who wishes to make a chair as a gift. The determination to make the chair is the final cause. Even though it is final, logically it is the first step. This goal of making a chair determines the material cause, wood, and the efficient cause, the carpenter. The wood and the carpenter in turn bring about the formal cause, the four-legged shape of the chair. In the end, there is a chair, "caused" by the four causes.

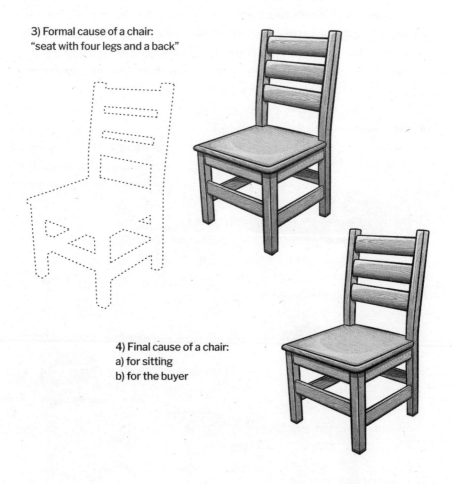

3) Formal cause of a chair:
"seat with four legs and a back"

4) Final cause of a chair:
a) for sitting
b) for the buyer

14

Aristotle's Categories

What is it? This is an all too familiar question whose answers allow for a wide range of possibilities. We can describe an octopus, for example, as an "animal," or as "small," or as "intelligent," depending on different contexts or different purposes. In some sense this very simple process is essential to our way of thinking and so to how philosophy is done as well.

What we think and how we think are shaped by the definitions we give, the distinctions we make, and the differences that matter. All of these aspects are represented in the way that we categorize the world around us. Categorization is at its root nothing more than grouping things together by likeness, a way to sort things together that are alike, and to distinguish these from those that are unlike. A common example of categorization is the allocation of a store into various areas stocked and sold with labels such as "baked goods," "dairy," "pasta," and so forth. Although it would strike us as odd, food could be sorted in an entirely different fashion, such as breakfast, lunch, and dinner, or by the curious, but consistent, method of size, with small foods in one section and the larger in another. This shows well enough that the concepts expressed in categorization arise as the result of how the world is and how we think of the world.

Aristotle is considered the father of disciplines such as biology and logic, areas in which categorization is essential.

THE ORIGIN OF CATEGORIES: A NEED TO CLASSIFY

Aristotle (384–322 BCE) was interested in categorization, to clarify, to understand, and to specify the things in the world. This is in a way the task of philosophy, but in a more primary sense categorization is preparatory to philosophy. Many scholars have speculated that the way Aristotle came up with his particular system of categorization was by asking the very question this chapter began with: "What is it?" Aristotle was very much pursuing this in a general way. There is a scientific methodology to the whole process, in that kinds of things are pursued rather than particular things. If Aristotle were applying his categorial theory to Socrates standing before him, he would say not that "Socrates" is what is before him, but a "man." A "man" is the type of thing that Socrates is. As we will see, categorization is more comprehensive than this answer indicates.

THE TEN CATEGORIES

Aristotle offered up ten categories: substance, quantity, quality, relative to, place, time, position, having, acting, being passive. Although he does not say so, these ten categories exhaust the way things can be in the

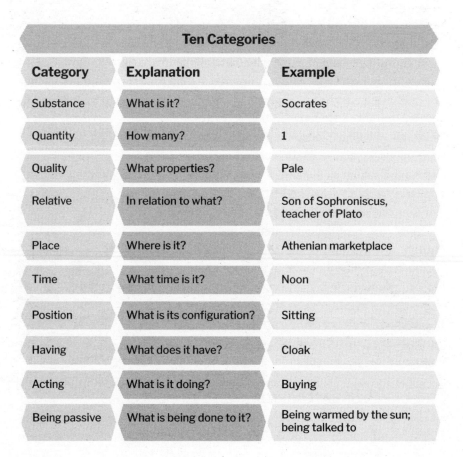

Ten Categories		
Category	**Explanation**	**Example**
Substance	What is it?	Socrates
Quantity	How many?	1
Quality	What properties?	Pale
Relative	In relation to what?	Son of Sophroniscus, teacher of Plato
Place	Where is it?	Athenian marketplace
Time	What time is it?	Noon
Position	What is its configuration?	Sitting
Having	What does it have?	Cloak
Acting	What is it doing?	Buying
Being passive	What is being done to it?	Being warmed by the sun; being talked to

world. There is no other way that something can be placed in a category outside of these ten. Furthermore these ten are the most general way of capturing what it is to be something. The categories are ultimate in that there is no other category under which these ten categories can themselves be categorized.

Some of the ten categories are understandable by their names alone, such as *when*, identifying the time at which something is happening, will happen, or has happened. Others are more difficult, such as *substance*, perhaps the most important category. However, before we examine the details of the individual categories, we should first look at one other element that the categories have in common. This is the concept of genus and species. This is not the same concept as the biological naming convention created by Charles Linnaeus, who was in fact modeling himself after Aristotle. In a nutshell, Aristotle's idea is that within every general type of thing, there are variations and sub-types. To leave Aristotle for a moment, it is quite easy to see that if we call "candy" a genus, there are many "species" of candy: lollipops, candy bars, chewing gum, jelly beans, marshmallows, and so forth. All are equally candy, answering to the genus of candy, but nevertheless they differ from each other while remaining candy. Aristotle calls the factor which makes for the difference of one thing from another the *differentia* (plural *differentiae*). So if all candy is "sugary confection," the differentiae of marshmallow would be its distinctive shape and texture. A marshmallow is a distinct species of its genus, candy, because of these differentiae of shape and texture. If candy is a sugary confection, then a marshmallow is a soft, white, cylindrical sugary confection.

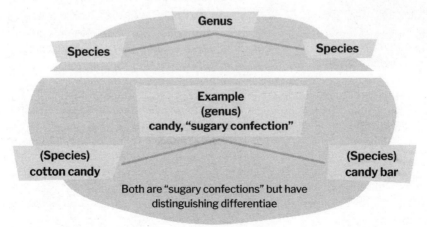

65

USING SOCRATES AS AN EXAMPLE FOR ARISTOTLE'S CATEGORIES

Now as we return to the specific characters of the ten categories, let us imagine that Socrates is sitting before us in Ancient Athens. His *substance* will be man, and his *quantity* will be 1 or single, his *quality* (among others) is pale, and his *relative* category, or *relation*, is (among others) son of Sophroniscus. Relation need not be confined to familial relations; we could just as easily designate "teacher of Plato" as another valid instance of the relative category. As for *place*, let's say we are all in the Athenian marketplace and the time is noon. Place and *time*, as well as other categories, are easily adjusted to be more or less precise. We could say "Greece," or "the earth," if we wanted to be more general, or "in front of the pottery stall" to be more specific. Even within the category of substance, but within limitations, we can be more or less general, in saying that Socrates is a "man" or an "animal" (with the understanding, of course, that a man is a species of animal). Continuing with the rest of the categories, the *position* of Socrates is sitting, since he is in a chair, and his *having* is having, in this instance also wearing, a shabby old cloak. In terms of acting or his activity, we can say Socrates is buying some food or engaging in discussion, and as for *being passive*, or what he is subject to, he is being warmed by the sun and talked to by passers-by.

We can apply Aristotle's ten categories to the philosopher Socrates, and by doing so, we can build up a picture of what it means to be Socrates.

Understanding all the categories gives us a holistic picture of what something is—in this case, what it is to be Socrates on a day long ago. The concept of the category is meant to capture something objective and scientific about the object we are investigating, and to guide our thought as we start with a comprehensive understanding of that object.

15

The Stoic Elimination of Emotion

Are emotions bad? Not individual emotions such as anger, which we might think negative or otherwise undesirable, but all emotions? If you could eliminate the emotions, would you? Is this even possible?

The Stoics, a philosophical school begun in Athens by Zeno of Citium (334–262 BCE), affirmed all of the above, advocating for the elimination of the emotions, or passions, because they were all considered bad. In this chapter we will analyze what the emotions are and exactly how this understanding informs the Stoic position. The Stoics' understanding of the emotions also gave them insight into how to reduce and eventually eliminate the emotions.

WHAT IS AN EMOTION?

To begin with, a passion or emotion—in Greek, *pathos*—is not too far removed in Greek philosophical economy from our own understanding of the term. The Greek word, like the English "passion," is derived from a word emphasizing the passive nature of emotion. This distinguishes emotions from activities on the one hand, and also brings out that an emotion, as a reaction, comes to be elicited by something external, some provocation or occasion which gives rise to the passion.

Zeno of Citium thought that emotions were strongly influenced by, and even determined by, beliefs.

67

Categorization of the Passions		
	Good	**Bad**
Present	present good: pleasure	present bad: distress
Future	future good: desire	future bad: fear

THE FOUR DIMENSIONS OF EMOTIONS

The passions are categorized along four different dimensions. These are good, bad, present, and future. The passion concerning a present good is pleasure, that of a future good a desire. The two passions which perceive the bad are distress (which is the bad when present) and fear (which is the bad that will come in the future). Pleasure takes eating an ice cream cone as a present good thing, while fear takes death as a future evil, for example. It needs to be kept in mind that this categorization of the passions is determined from the perspective of how we view certain things. That is, we may have a desire of some future good, like a holiday, but this does not mean the desire itself is good, at least according to the Stoics, but only that we perceive the holiday as a good. There are other sub-kinds of emotions in addition to the list above, but they can all be fitted into one of the four categories. As has already been stated, the aim of the Stoic is to eliminate every last one of these emotions.

EMOTIONS ARE NOT VIRTUOUS

The passions are an unwelcome intrusion in the Stoic system. The overriding reason is that the only necessity for happiness in the Stoic mind is virtue. Virtue, on their understanding, had no room for the passions. What is it, then, that made the passions so unsavory to the Stoics? In brief, emotions were viewed at odds with virtue because the emotions reflect a view of something as valuable, when nothing except virtue is valuable. Emotions are built upon beliefs, and it is these beliefs which bestow on emotions the power they possess. In contrast to how we view emotions today, the Stoic denied that emotions are a state of mind which just happens to us as humans, that we are blameless and without agency in how our emotions manifest. Emotions get their start through belief, and it is this belief which explains the badness of emotions.

The Stoics claim that emotions have mental content, and emotions indicate and promote belief in anyone who has them. To start, emotions make a claim about value. That is, as we saw in the four dimensions described on the previous page, emotions ascribe to an object or activity goodness or badness. There is a fear of death, because we judge death to be bad, not good. This mental process which culminates in a judgment about goodness or badness can be put in a propositional form, such as "death is bad." Furthermore, this value judgment is out of proportion to the actual value of the object or activity under consideration. Earlier we saw that Stoics value only virtue; not only is virtue sufficient for happiness, but it is virtue alone which we should value and desire. Virtue is held so high that the Stoics maintain that a virtuous man is still happy even when being tortured. So the standard to which the Stoics are holding our judgments about what is good or bad is virtue itself. If the object of our concern is not virtue, we should not care about it. If we do care about death (as something bad) or money (as something good), we are attaching to death or money a value which it does not have, since the loyalty of our value should be given to virtue alone. To fear death is to overvalue death, and to desire money is to overvalue money. Virtue is and ought to be our overriding human concern.

The Emotions Indicate Judgments of Value

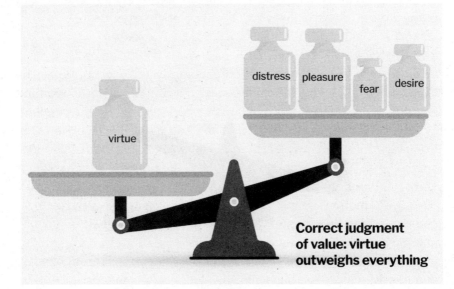

distress pleasure fear desire

virtue

Correct judgment
of value: virtue
outweighs everything

BEING UPSET BY WHAT IS UNIMPORTANT

We have now seen that the Stoic attack on the emotions hinges on how the emotions make a claim on our values and hence our beliefs. Thus when we become distressed at getting a deep, unwashable food stain on our favorite shirt, the pain of this distress is not merely an unavoidable effect forcing itself upon us, like a biological reaction. This distress about the shirt is undergirded by certain beliefs about the shirt and the relation of the shirt to ourselves. We overvalue the shirt, thinking it something which is valuable when it is not. And we misjudge the relation the shirt bears to the status of ourselves as possessors, or not, of virtue. The entirety of this process of emotion is built upon a false foundation of ascribing value to things which should not be valued. In this sense, emotions are *rational*. Rational not in the sense of "what ought to be decided by the mind," but in the general sense of being the outcome of some process of deliberation and choice, decided and evaluated by the mind.

What we have seen is that the Stoics considered emotions bad because they contained, or we could even say "encoded," a false belief about how the world is—in particular, a value attached to anything besides virtue itself. In the end, the emotions are undesirable because quite literally they are not virtuous.

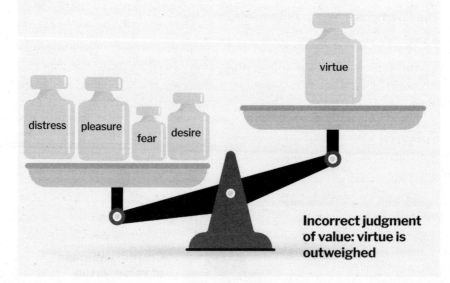

distress pleasure fear desire

virtue

Incorrect judgment of value: virtue is outweighed

16
The Idea of Existence

Is is arguably our most familiar concept. "This tea is bad," "The man is my brother," "I don't know where my jacket is," "Purple is a beautiful color." It is so familiar that we can hardly say or think anything without it (including the beginning of this sentence, where it slipped by you). But like the familiar concept of time, its analysis tends to confuse us.

There is a strong sense of *is*, one which we use to talk about whether something substantially exists. We think that we *are*, and that the world *is* in this strong existential sense. So we believe that some things exist. But what does this mean, for something to exist? Is existence something in its own right?

If we look back to the beginning of the discussion about existence in Western philosophy, it begins with Ancient Greece. Existence and non-existence were sources of fascinated speculation for many philosophers during this time. It was in the philosophy of Plato (428–348 BCE) and Aristotle (384–322 BCE) that thinking about existence reached a mature form.

ARISTOTLE AND THE ACTIVITY OF BEING

Aristotle believed that for something to exist means for it to be what it is. So far, this does not seem helpful. But there is more to the statement than there appears. If we ask of Spot what he is essentially, the most immediately available explanation is that he is a dog. Spot exists as a dog. One could go further and ask what a dog is most essentially, and the answer would be an animal—or, if we continue further, asking what an animal is, we could answer a certain combination of fire, air, water, and earth. This process of nested answers will eventually stop at the category of substance itself. We cannot appeal to what substance is, because in Aristotle's view, dogs and other substances are simply

**Aristotle:
existence is what a thing is**

A dog is:
- a dog
- an animal
- a combination of fire, earth, air, and
  water (i.e. elements)

substances; there is no higher category, such as existence, to which one
can appeal as an explanation.

AQUINAS: EXISTENCE AND ESSENCE

Thomas Aquinas (1225–74 CE), following a tradition at least as early as the
philosopher Boethius (477–524 CE), made a distinction between existence
and essence. A starting point for this distinction is the acknowledgement
that things come into being and also perish. In normal cases like animals,
plants, or even objects like houses or tables, there is a process where
first these things come to be and then they pass out of existence. Tables
can exist or not; but the definition of a table, its essence, is distinct from
whether a table exists or not. When considering the idea of coming to
be and perishing, Aquinas argued that since God did not come into
being or perish, and this is true of God alone, existence and essence are
identical in God. In the case of material things like a table, the essence
of the table is expressed through the physical form of the table's shape.
In this particular example we might say the essence of a table is a "flat
surface with four legs." As soon as this physical instantiation of the table
is destroyed—by a crack right down the middle, say—then the table
ceases to exist as a table. (It still continues to exist as two large pieces of
wood, or a combination of atoms.)

FREGE: THREE USES OF "IS"

Gottlob Frege (1848–1925), a mathematician and philosopher, offered
some important distinctions in the concept of existence by examining
the word *is*. There are three different ways to understand this word,
and if we do not acknowledge these different uses, then we are bound
to end in confusion, thinking that each of these uses straightforwardly

means *exist*. There is the *is* of identity, such as when we say "Paris is the capital of France." One thing is being equated with, or simply identified, as the second thing. There is the *is* of predication such as "My dog is brown." Someone is claiming in such a statement not that brown is the same thing as her dog, but that her dog has the property of being brown. Lastly comes the *is* of existence, which is distinguished from these first two examples, such as in the claim "God is."

IS EXISTENCE A PROPERTY?

In addition to analysis over *is*, another issue in the philosophical discussions over existence which has proved to be controversial is whether the use of *exists* is in fact a property. That is, if we say "Samantha exists," are we making a statement about what belongs to Samantha? Some notable philosophers have believed that existence is not a property. This might sound like a mere semantic quibble, but there is at least one good reason why we could be persuaded to deny that existence is a property. Suppose Samantha dies. Now can we say that "Samantha does not exist"? We make negative claims about existence in this way all the time, it seems, so there should be no problem: "That store no longer exists," "The Roman Empire does not exist." If we want to preserve the truth of these statements, then we must deny that existence is a property, according to what we may call these "anti-property" proponents. On their view, if existence were a property, what we are saying when we say "Samantha

Boethius: one of the earlier medieval Latin thinkers was a theologian and philosopher who distinguished betweem existence and essence.

73

does not exist," is simultaneously positing that something exists and does not exist. If anything worries philosophers, it is asserting something and its negation at the same time—a contradiction in its pure form.

Another worry if we say that existence is a property is the question of what it adds to a thing. This may be strange, you think, since to add existence to something simply means that it is here in reality along with us, rather than not. However, consider the statement that "The soft pillow exists." We think we know what this means. But to be "soft" means that something is already in reality—it is not possible to be soft (or hard for that matter) in the abstract or in a state of non-existence. To be soft—for a pillow, a bed, or a ripe peach—those objects must already exist.

Type	Example
Predication	The tree is green.
Identification	Paris is the capital of France.
Existence	God is.

17

The Existence of the Divine

"Does God exist?" has probably been thought many more times than it has been uttered out loud. The question is simple yet profound, and is arguably the most important question that can be asked. The question itself can be interpreted neutrally, as a genuine indication of curiosity, but also as a skeptical prod: there cannot really be a God, can there?

In his work *Summa Theologica*, Thomas Aquinas (1225–74) was addressing this exact question over God's existence. The method of the *Summa* is to posit questions and give answers in the context of objections and replies. In this discussion over God's existence, the objections Aquinas has in mind are the problem of evil, or how there can be a God when there is evil in the world, as well as how God seems to be unnecessary. The second objection amounts to the belief that natural causes alone can account for the state of the world.

In this chapter we will explore the case Aquinas made for the existence of God. Traditionally this section of the *Summa* has been called the Five Ways for the five brief arguments he introduces. Although the ideas are in some ways Aquinas's unique formulation, in another sense he was building upon older arguments for the existence of God, especially as seen in Aristotle (384–322 BCE).

THE FIRST WAY: MOTION

The first way is the argument from motion. Aquinas says that whatever is in motion must be moved by something else in motion. It is hard to disagree with this. However, the fact that everything that moves has an external source of motion needs to be supplemented with some other ideas so that this can lead to the idea of God. One assumption is that

St Thomas Aquinas, the quintessential philosopher and theologian of the Middle Ages. He synthesized ancient philosophy and Christian revelation.

nothing in the world can move itself. Something may have a kind of self-motion, as a human who can move herself wherever she chooses, but this is not what Aquinas has in mind. Staying with the same example, he is instead saying that a person is obviously not the cause of her own motion because it is evident that she was created at a certain time, and was obviously not moving herself before that time, and arguably not even moving herself in the womb. So there must be some prior set of motions to which we can turn. Even though each motion must be set off by another in turn, this cannot go on forever. It has to stop somewhere. This, says Aquinas, is God, who sets off the entire chain of movement by moving other things but not himself being moved.

THE SECOND WAY: EFFICIENT CAUSE

The second way is very similar to the argument of the first. It relies on the concept of the *efficient cause*, an idea borrowed from Aristotle. An efficient cause, for the purposes of the argument, is anything that causes something else to come into being. So a father is the efficient cause of a child and, in a more extended sense, the sun is the efficient cause of a seed sprouting into a plant. The efficient cause brings about a change in being. Along with every efficient cause comes the result or effect which it brings about. Just as the child cannot be the efficient cause of himself, so more generally things cannot be their own efficient cause. In other words, everything which comes to be must be caused by an efficient cause external to itself, and yet this process cannot go back forever. The process has to regress back in time somewhere. This leaves God as the first efficient cause.

Existence of God

The argument from motion

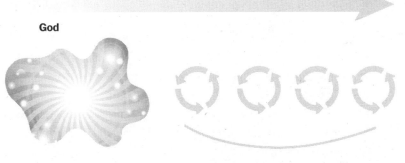

God

As creator
moves others, but is not moved

Parts of creation
move others and are themselves moved

THE THIRD WAY: POSSIBILITY AND NECESSITY

The third way is perhaps the most difficult, and is the most abstract. It is an argument based on possibility and necessity. The idea is that the universe we see around us is clearly corruptible. Everything comes into being and perishes eventually. Aquinas words it this way: that it is possible for all things to exist and not exist. But if it is possible for all things not to exist, then it clearly is also possible for all things not to have existed in the past. This would mean nothing existed in the past, but this is a problem in that nothing has no power to become something, because it is nothing. And since there are obviously things existing in the world now, it is clear that some agent caused the world to come into being out of nothing. The conclusion is that the agent who did this is God, since nothing did not have the power of doing this by itself.

The argument from efficient cause

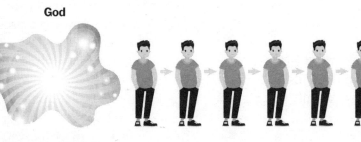

God

God does not come to be, so he does not need a cause

Everything that comes to be needs a cause

The argument from possibility and necessity

God

At some point in
the past nothing
existed

Now things exist

Nothing cannot make itself into
something, so God must have
begun the process of making
something

THE FOURTH WAY: THE HIGHEST AND BEST

Aquinas's fourth way appeals to the gradations of qualities we observe in the world. When we speak of qualities in this world, we speak of "more or less," such as something being more or less hot. We judge the concept of hotness itself by that which we think is the hottest thing, fire. Thus when we talk about the good, the true, and the noble, we are comparing this to something which is best, truest, and noblest. As in the case of fire, which causes all other hot things to have their heat, so the best, truest, and noblest causes all other things to be good, true, and noble. The best, truest, and noblest being is God.

The argument from gradations

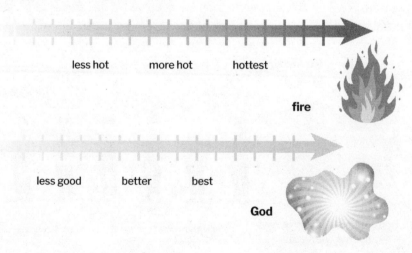

less hot   more hot   hottest

fire

less good   better   best

God

THE FIFTH WAY: THE DESIGN OF THE UNIVERSE

The fifth way depends on the order and governance of the world. The world is intelligent and intelligible. Aquinas does not have in mind the actions and creations of humans, or even animals, when he speaks of intelligence. What he means is that the world displays regularity and consistency in its very makeup, even in things which lack a mind. For instance, even a simple thing, like a stone, always falls back down to the earth when it is tossed in the air. Aquinas argues that the regularity of the stone and other natural objects and laws like it display an intelligence by seeking out and attaining their goal, such as the stone does in landing and staying on the earth. But intelligence has to belong to some intelligent being which causes the stone and all other similar things to behave as they do, and this intelligent being is nothing other than God himself.

The argument from governance

The natural world shows evidence of regular, natural order such as rocks always falling downwards.

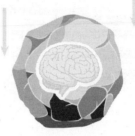

But rocks do not have minds, unlike plants or animals. Therefore, God, as intelligent creator, must be behind this rational order.

18

The Possibility
of Miracles

**Miracles are almost synonymous with hope, or with the pains
of desperation. We "hold out" for a miracle as much as we
"pray for" a miracle. To have a miracle occur is almost beyond
belief. In some ways, expecting a miracle means that we
are not expecting a miracle at all, for miracles are not to be
expected.**

To believe in the miraculous is to believe in the supernatural, and in the
minds of many this requires bringing in the idea of God. This association
is more pronounced when a given religion claims that specific and historic
miracles are proof of a divine revelation, such as Jesus walking on water
or his resurrection. Although we might be confident we could recognize
a miracle, what would our method of detection be?

RECOGNIZING A MIRACLE FROM EXPERIENCE
If you saw that a friend was unexpectedly and nearly spontaneously
healed from a serious disease, against all medical prognostication, would
you consider a miracle as the possible cause? This kind of scenario is
a good place to start, for it brings to mind the contrast that is at the
heart of a miracle. On the one hand is the normal course of the world
as we expect it, fashioned in our minds from years of experience and
observation. This experience often encompasses our whole life, so that if
something violates our expectation, our first reaction is likely to include
shock and disbelief. On the other hand is the putative miracle itself,
whose distinct character is so at odds with experience as to produce
our perplexed reaction. Whatever else it is, a miracle is a profoundly
psychological event, which disrupts our view of the world as a baseline
of consistency.

THE PRECONDITIONS FOR A MIRACLE

If a miracle is not ruled out as an impossibility from the outset, there are one and possibly two assumptions for a miracle to be credible to us. The first concerns the means through which a miracle is supposed to be perceived by us. The observance of a miracle is open to us in the same way as anything else on the earth, through our eyes and ears and other senses. The degree to which we find our senses to be reliable and faithful reporters is the degree to which we can trust them. If our eyes are prone, for example, to see things that are not there, then this would be a reason to doubt any particular instance of an apparent miracle.

A second consideration is the existence of someone or something which intervenes in the normal course of affairs. There could be some exotic possibility such as a race of advanced alien life responsible for miracles, but the usual explanation is that some divinity is behind a miracle, an agent who performs an unexpected action for a unique purpose. This understanding is reflected in the phrase *divine intervention* as a synonym for miracle. Although I have presented an appeal to the divine as an assumption for the miraculous to occur, the relationship can also lead from the miraculous to the divine. Just as the concept of a miracle can presume the existence of divinity, it also can be the case that a miracle is used as evidence for the existence of the divine.

HUME'S OPPOSITION TO MIRACLES

This is a good point at which to explore the skeptical position toward miracles. David Hume (1711–76) also saw a close connection between the divine, in particular religious claims, and miracles. In fact, he thought the only good reason to subscribe to any religious system is the appearance of miracles. The problem, however, is that miracles are either impossible, unlikely, or, perhaps worst of all, unable to be verified.

The brunt of Hume's objection to miracles is tied up in the notion of natural laws. If there are natural laws, these have been established

Preconditions for believing a miracle

A An ability to distinguish a miracle from a non-miracle.

B A trust in the senses (or the reports) which observe the miracle.

C An attribution or source for the miracle, a miracle maker such as God.

David Hume is famous today for his skepticism about miracles, causation, and religion in general.

by a repeated and consistent observation over time. For instance, when someone dies, we see that he stays dead. Have you ever personally, Hume could say, seen someone recover from death? From his perspective, whatever arguments and evidence could be brought forth in favor of a miracle would be vastly outweighed by the incredible amount of evidence that shows the steadfastness of a natural law. So if there is a claim that someone who died came back to life, this is a single instance as compared with the millions or billions of people who have died and stayed dead. The safe bet would be to say that the claim of a miracle is mistaken in some way, as an illusion or an erroneous judgment that the person was dead in the first place.

There is somewhat of a stalemate in these two approaches to miracles, with believers on one side and skeptics on the other. It is a philosophical disagreement much more than a dispute about the kind and quantity of evidence. For the unique and unprecedented character of a miracle is what makes it a miracle for the believer and what disqualifies it as a possibility for the skeptic.

A RETURN TO MIRACLES AND EXPERIENCE

As a final part of the discussion, we will consider the way in which miracles can be known and discovered. The problem arises because of our experience. Suppose we judge something to be a miracle based on our experience of the natural world. It follows that if we have formed an incomplete or wrong understanding, our perception of a miracle may be brought into question. Consider the example of someone who has lived on a tropical and remote island all his life, far from the influence of modernity. His tribe is unfamiliar with ice since it is never cold. A ship finds the island and introduces ice to the man, and he thinks that ice is a miracle since water has been turned solid. The man would be justified in thinking this a miracle. This would be an argument not so much against miracles as against our ability to discern them. One thing this shows is that we should be very careful in what we call a miracle, and that the designation of something as a miracle depends to a large degree on our naming it as such and assuming we know what it looks like.

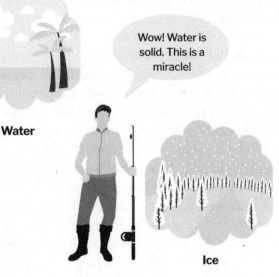

Water is always liquid.

An islander who never saw ice before would be justified in thinking it a miracle.

Wow! Water is solid. This is a miracle!

Water

Ice

19

Design in the Natural Universe

Suppose you are walking along the seashore one night and see some object catching the reflection of the moonlight. As you approach and pick it up, you see that it is a rather handsome pocket watch. You might have several questions.

Where did it come from? Whose is it? How much is it worth? However fascinated you are, all of your questions about the watch would depend on something even more fundamental. This would be the belief that what you are examining did not spontaneously come to be, like a mushroom sprouting from ether. Nor has the watch always been sitting there as an everlasting and fundamental feature of the seashore. You would take it for granted that someone made this pocket watch to tell the time. The watch is an object of an intelligent human mind, not a chance occurrence of metal and glass.

GOD AS THE WATCHMAKER

If the above line of reasoning is immediately appealing to you, as it is and has been to many others over the centuries, then there is a second step which is often made, where the argument is transferred to the case for God's existence as creator in light of the evident creation seen around us. There is an analogy or comparison drawn directly from the case of products of intelligence, like watches or music, to the case of the universe as a whole. If a watch requires a creator, then likewise the universe requires a creator. This argument for the existence of God has been called the argument from design or the teleological argument, teleology signifying a Greek concept about the arrangement towards order, to which the argument draws our attention.

A very similar argument to the watchmaker argument above was

Are both designed?

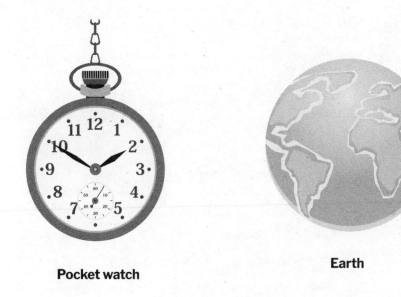

Pocket watch

Earth

put forth by William Paley (1743–1805). But the argument goes much further back than this. Plato (428–348 BCE), for instance, in the tenth book of his *Laws*, argues that the complexity of the cosmos visible at night is sufficient to cause belief in the gods. In his lost book *On Philosophy*, Aristotle (384–322 BCE) concurs with this judgment, imagining a people sequestered underground their entire lives, and when emerging to see the sky for the first time being struck and provoked by wonder into believing that the gods exist.

VARIOUS KINDS OF DESIGN

This argument has caught the attention of many people for its simplicity and the ease with which it can be conveyed to others. This does not mean it is not sophisticated, however. An indication of this is the various forms the argument has taken. So, for instance, the argument may be no more than a broad analogy between design and the world, or it may argue for certain hallmarks of intelligence seen in both human-crafted products and the world. It may claim that the universe as a whole indicates design, or offer a particular aspect of the world for consideration, such as the molecular intricacies of biological cells, the arrangement of the planetary systems, or the finely tuned ecological circumstances of the world seemingly designed for human occupation.

William Paley set out teleological arguments for the existence of God in his book Natural Theology.

The design argument, some think, goes beyond merely making a parallel between what are obvious cases of design, like watches, and the natural world, which they also argue is designed. The idea is that the design we see in the natural world actually exceeds that seen in the realm of human production. The universe has more indications of complexity and intelligence in it than a mere pocket watch. If a pocket watch is designed, and we can be sure that it is designed, then how much more confident can we be that the universe itself was designed by a creator?

THE QUALITY OF DESIGN

If we look more closely at the teleological argument, we can tease out several different elements. To begin with, there is an appeal to complexity. Just as there is sophistication seen in an automobile or computer, there is sophistication in the natural world around us. There is also an integration of parts for the functioning of the whole. As gears and cogs are in the function of the watch, so we might understand the biological ecosystem working to regulate and maintain life forms and the world they inhabit. Perhaps most controversial would be the claim that just as the watch is "for" something, namely telling time to a person, so the universe, by virtue of it being created, has a purpose or goal, often understood as aligning with the purposes of God.

APPEARANCE AND DESIGN

There is an undeniable element of "you know it when you see it" to uncontroversial examples of design, even when the design is shoddy and elementary, such as a young child's finger painting. One conclusion we can derive from this is that a design argument depends on appearance to some degree. One way of formulating this is that everything that is designed appears to be designed, but there is dispute about whether everything that appears to be designed is designed.

INTELLIGENT DESIGN

A modern-day version of the teleological argument has emerged in the controversial "intelligent design" movement. The argument so far has been applied only to the microscopic level of biology, although it could theoretically be used in other fields. Sensing that the theory of evolution threatens the appearance of design in the universe, proponents have claimed that there are biological features that are "irreducibly complex." What does this mean? The thought is that we can conceive of a biological structure as an interlocking and functioning whole, whose parts cannot

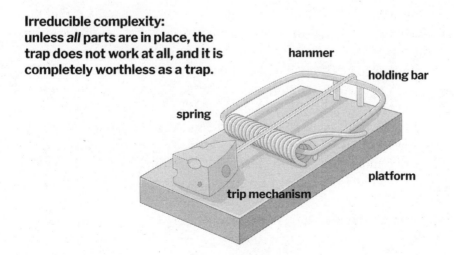

**Irreducible complexity:
unless *all* parts are in place, the
trap does not work at all, and it is
completely worthless as a trap.**

hammer

holding bar

spring

platform

trip mechanism

be isolated from each other. Each part must be in place simultaneously and if the parts are not so arranged, the feature is entirely useless. Imagine taking the spring or hammer, or the strip of wood, away from a common mousetrap. It's not that this device, missing one or more of these parts, is a poor or worse mousetrap than one with them: it fails to be a mousetrap at all. The conclusion is there cannot be a cumulative and gradual process of development (such as evolution) from the simple to the complex. Rather, one must invoke a creator as the explanation.

20
Good and Evil

Our immediate conception of thinking of good and bad is likely to bring up images of a battle between forces of light and darkness, what is wrong and right, and even God and the devil. Our ethical lives, whatever beliefs we subscribe to, have in common an adherence to the good.

At least, it is difficult to find people who openly admit (if we would then even believe them) that they seek out what is evil and live by evil rather than the good. Good is our guiding light, that which we seem to aim toward—and those actions and events which we most disapprove of, we deem bad or even evil.

THE LANDSCAPE OF GOOD AND EVIL

A first step to understanding good and evil is that *good* and *evil* are used in many ways. Perhaps the most important is the ethical sense, in which we appraise things as good or evil in accordance with some moral value. An equally important aspect is a conception of *good* and *evil* almost as things proper in themselves, distinct from our own conceptions and labels, entities which have an independent existence as part of truths about the universe.

TWO KINDS OF EVIL

Evil has traditionally been divided into two kinds. *Moral* evils are brought about, indirectly or directly, by human agents. *Natural* evils are distinguished by an origin distinct from human agency, such as earthquakes and diseases. Both evils are to be avoided, but this distinction of moral evil allows us to focus on humans as causes of evil, to be condemned appropriately.

The acknowledgement of natural evil has led some philosophers to doubt that evil really exists outside of our imagination. An earthquake,

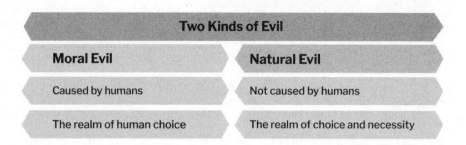

Two Kinds of Evil	
Moral Evil	**Natural Evil**
Caused by humans	Not caused by humans
The realm of human choice	The realm of choice and necessity

for example, has no intrinsic evil quality. If there are earthquakes on Mars, which is unpeopled, we do not think the shifting of tectonic plates on that planet is a natural evil, or indeed any other kind of evil. It is only because there is a direct relation and interest to human affairs that we deem an earthquake evil.

In considering the relation of human activity to good and evil, some have thought that this analysis of natural evil ought to be extended to moral evil as well. Just as there is nothing evil in natural catastrophes, so there is no evil in what we call moral evils, for what we are expressing is dismay over how something affects us personally, whether this comes about from nature or human agency. Despite this, we might think that the personal nature of how evil affects us is exactly what makes it what it is. It is because evil is something which thwarts, disrupts, or destroys moral agents that it is the kind of thing that should be shunned.

Earthquakes are a form of natural evil and so have no relation to human agency, which can be a benefit or drawback in explaining them.

THE NATURE OF GOOD AND EVIL

If there is such a thing as good or evil, what could explain their nature? The abstract nature of good and evil has led many to the conclusion that no definition of either is possible. For a first approach at defining good, we might look to a dictionary, which tells us that good is what is suitable or fit. From this we can extrapolate two relevant details—who or what it is suitable for, and in what this suitability consists. If a car tyre is good, it is good for driving and this is its suitability. It is also good for the driver, and this is who it is suitable for. In this analysis there are many different kinds and applications, and so definitions, of what is good. This leaves us still wanting a general account of the good. A similar vagueness arises if we define the good as that which is pleasurable or desirable. Although it is true that what is good is good for someone and for a particular purpose, and that the good is desirable and pleasant, this description strikes us as rather unhelpful, since all of these conditions could be fulfilled by someone who was doing what we would consider to be evil.

HOW DO GOOD AND EVIL RELATE TO EACH OTHER?

Evil and good, as we noted at the beginning, are often associated with each other. There is a way in which we best approach the knowledge of what each is by contrasting it with the other. One understanding of good and evil lies within the framework of *dualism*. Dualism is the belief that

Yin and yang

good and bad are two opposed forces, each battling for supremacy. Even though good and evil are each trying to get the upper hand, as seen in the vicissitudes of human life, this is ultimately impossible since they are equal and necessary components of the world. Dualism can have a strong religious orientation, as can be seen in Manichaeism or Taoism. In Taoism one can see in yin and yang a holistic concept that parallels the role of good and bad in dualism.

Plotinus said evil had no existence by itself, but was the absence of good.

An alternative to explaining good and evil, while still depending on the intimate relationship between the two, is understanding good as the primary and essential element, with evil as a derivative feature dependent on good for both its existence and definition. This conception of evil was first offered by the Greek philosopher Plotinus (204–270 CE). Plotinus thought that evil was a non-entity in that it was a mere privation. Evil cannot stand on its own but is a lack of the relevant substance or property under investigation. Plotinus held that the privation seen in evil is absolute; it is a complete lack and this is what accounts for its evil. St Augustine (354–430 CE), taking this model, described sickness as an example of evil, being the privation of health, and vice as the privation of virtue.

Good and evil are concepts at once primal and essential to how we do and do not want to live. Perhaps the most significant philosophical question about good and evil is whether knowing about them will help us in any way to be good and avoid evil. Life must often be lived in the particular and actions are the particulars of life. If we are to find good and evil in anything but the abstract, it is in our actions that we will find them.

21

The Nature of Knowledge

Knowledge is almost always associated with the positive: wisdom, education, ability, intelligence, insight. But this approach takes for granted that there is something called knowledge and that we actually possess it. There is a deeper, and we might even say darker, aspect to knowledge. This is the knowledge of knowledge.

When we begin to explore and examine what we know, an entirely new horizon of concerns comes into view. Is there knowledge? How do I know what I know? Why do I believe what I believe? Can I explain and justify my thoughts, to myself and also to others? The exploration of these and other questions can be exhilarating, but also overpowering, forcing us to consider our beliefs from the ground up, tempting us to abandon our beliefs for guarded skepticism, or to give up hope of ever attaining wisdom.

WHAT DOES THE STUDY OF KNOWLEDGE COVER?

Epistemology, or the study of knowledge, is an expansive and ever-expanding field within philosophy. Although knowledge is the chief goal in this enterprise, epistemology as such is concerned with more than just knowledge, if we consider knowledge as the highest or surest level of cognitive attainment.

A PRIORI AND *A POSTERIORI* KNOWLEDGE

Given the enormous scope of human investigation into knowledge, there is a corresponding diversity of different types of knowledge, of which only some of the most important can be listed here. *A priori* knowledge is knowledge that literally comes via experience "from before." Thus knowledge that 2 and 2 is 4, or that "a bachelor is an unmarried man" are both forms of this knowledge. Saying that a bachelor is an unmarried

Type of Knowledge	Relation to Experience	Example
A priori	Acquired independent of experience	Bachelors are unmarried men
A posteriori	Acquired as a result of experience	Paris is the capital of France

man simply appeals to the definition of "bachelor," so there is no need to go looking out into the world to confirm if each and every bachelor is in fact unmarried. *A posteriori* is knowledge that is acquired "from later"—that is, knowledge which comes about after one has experienced the world. Examples of this kind of knowledge are: "Winston Churchill was Prime Minister when World War II ended," "Paris is the capital of France," and "Owls are nocturnal animals." None of these could be known by the use of reason alone. In *a posteriori* knowledge there is a dependence on experience, which does not come into play with *a priori* knowledge.

KNOWLEDGE-THAT AND KNOWLEDGE-HOW
Another very helpful distinction in the analysis of knowledge is *knowledge-that* as contrasted with *knowledge-how*. *Knowledge-that* is knowledge about propositions. This is the kind of knowledge often associated with textbooks: facts, figures, concepts, definitions, and the like. These forms of knowledge can easily be described and explained in language and so are quite capable of being widely produced and known. In contrast, *knowledge-how* cannot be formulated so easily, and perhaps description in words only obscures its true character. This is knowledge of how to do things from the experiential perspective of the one who possesses it. Knowledge of how to juggle is a good example. If you do not know how to juggle, you could read every book ever written about how to

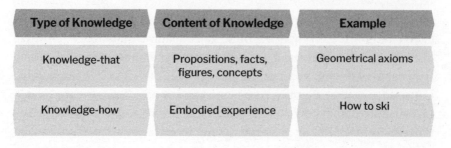

Type of Knowledge	Content of Knowledge	Example
Knowledge-that	Propositions, facts, figures, concepts	Geometrical axioms
Knowledge-how	Embodied experience	How to ski

Isaac Newton, or at least his thought, is still alive today, in the sense that physicists still use his insights to further knowledge.

juggle. Yet all the written knowledge declared in these books would not confer on you the ability to juggle. To juggle you actually have to be able to throw three balls into the air, a knowledge which will come about through time, labor, and many dropped balls. Even after you have learned how to juggle, you cannot in turn transfer this knowledge to someone else so that they are able to juggle immediately after hearing from you.

DISTRIBUTED KNOWLEDGE

We are used to thinking of the individual as the knower. But there are also types of knowing that apply to groups of people. One obvious example is the advance of science, which depends on the accumulation of knowledge over time. Sometimes the mature growth of this knowledge takes time, with the present building upon the advancements of the past. One example is the sense that present physicists must "borrow" from Isaac Newton to explain their own research. The knowledge they possess is shared across time. In addition to being shared across time, there are also times when knowledge is compartmentalized and distributed through many different people, each with knowledge limited to a specific area. For instance, in the production of a smartphone, there are people charged with making the electronic circuits, others who design and make the battery, others who design the physical appearance of the phone, and still others who create the user interface which the consumer will use to operate the phone. All of these areas are separated in that those working in each need only have a general knowledge of how the other areas work. There is no need for the battery producer to possess the technical knowledge of the computer programmer who designs the operating system of the phone. Yet it is only as a whole group of producers that the knowledge of how to produce a phone comes about.

SPECIALIZED AND GENERAL KNOWLEDGE

When thinking about specialized knowledge, we may come to think about the relation of specialized to general knowledge. Specialized knowledge has come to be valued for two main reasons. The first is that it has allowed for incredible advances in the application of knowledge, such as computers and cars. The second is that the structure of higher education has developed in such a way that it promotes knowledge within a narrow field to cater to the professional needs of the business community.

The role of general knowledge and its role in society is perhaps underappreciated if not overlooked. What is general knowledge, and how is such knowledge even possible in today's busy world? It is knowledge that seeks a broad, but not always in every area equally deep, knowledge about everything from how the world works to history, nature, science, and even how to understand. It is perhaps the desire to understand which is the most valuable knowledge to be found, for it is only when this knowledge has been acquired that all other knowledge becomes possible.

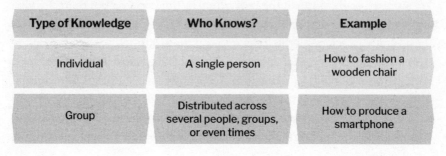

Type of Knowledge	Who Knows?	Example
Individual	A single person	How to fashion a wooden chair
Group	Distributed across several people, groups, or even times	How to produce a smartphone

22

The Existence of an Immortal Soul

A soul, by some accounts, is something we cannot see, touch, or feel. It wholly transcends the material world, beyond the taint of the corruptible. Why then should we mortals even care about souls? Well, many of the thinkers who have advocated for the existence of such a soul have also maintained that humans are, at their most fundamental level, souls.

But it is one thing to offer up an idea for what the soul might be, quite another to provide a convincing reason for thinking this to be so. However, if we are souls or think we might be, our concern will surely grow for investigating the existence of the soul. An important assumption of belief in this kind of soul is that the soul both accounts for our identity as persons and, insofar as it does this, is superior and preferable to the body.

THE IMMATERIAL SOUL
What perhaps turns out to be the most common appeal for the immortality of the soul also coincides with what is claimed as the unique property of the soul. This is its nature as something wholly non-material. This view—that the soul is distinct and of a different nature than what is physical in the human person—is called *substance dualism*. The soul understood in this way stands apart as something unique so that it is not vulnerable like the body, most significantly in death, but also in disease and illness.

THE PROPERTIES OF THE SOUL
One line of thought, going back at least as far as Cicero (106–43 BCE) and extending to Descartes (1596–1650 CE) and right up to the current day, is to emphasize the properties which the soul possesses. Among other abilities, the soul can comprehend anything, has a marvelous store of

René Descartes is probably the most famous exponent of an immaterial soul separate from a material body.

memories fitted into it, and has the ability to discover and create new things. Yet none of these properties, and more besides, can be explained in terms of the material. Matter, in principle, could never account for these wonderful attributes. How could oxygen or iron, which make up our bodies, or blood and bone, if we go up one level, ever give rise to the dynamic abilities of the soul? The center of this idea is a negative, but often successful, tactic. It is to show that such an idea of what we know a soul to be, with its fantastic mental qualities, can never be explained in purely physical terms.

PLATO ON THE SOUL

One of the most brilliant thinkers on the soul is Plato (428–348 BCE). He ascribes to the soul qualities such as immortality, immateriality, and even divinity. In his book *Phaedo*, written from the dramatic point of view of the impending death of Socrates, he develops several arguments for the immortality of the soul.

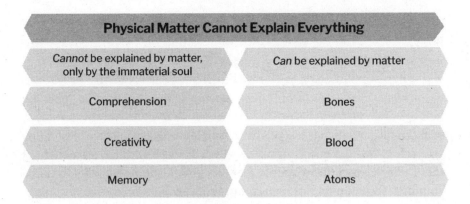

Physical Matter Cannot Explain Everything	
Cannot be explained by matter, only by the immaterial soul	*Can* be explained by matter
Comprehension	Bones
Creativity	Blood
Memory	Atoms

THE ARGUMENT FROM OPPOSITES

The first argument appeals to the difference alluded to above between the body and the soul. Body and soul are in one sense opposed to each other, different kinds of things, but in another sense a human has these two elements, body and soul. A human is a soul and body living harmoniously together. So there are two states of the human body: 1) the soul in a state in which it is connected to the body—life; 2) the soul in a state in which it is disconnected from the body—death. We will return in a moment to how life and death, defined in these ways, are important.

Socrates also makes the point that things, if and when they come about, come about from their opposites. So if something hot comes about, it was previously cold, or if someone comes to be awake, she was previously sleeping. This understanding of opposites is applied to everything, says Socrates, and as long as the world keeps going, opposites come to be from their opposites.

If all this is true, then the living come to be from the dead, says Socrates, since death is the opposite of life. As we saw above, being alive is the combination of soul and body, and death is the separation of soul from body. The culmination of this argument is an acknowledgement that we will come to die, which is the separation of soul and body. However, since opposites not only come from opposites, but opposites lead to other opposites, there will come a day when the separation of the body and soul, death, will lead to the reunion (combination) of body and soul, life. So although we die, we will one day live again.

DESCARTES: THE SOUL IS OUR TRUE SELF

Another distinction relying on the difference between the soul and body can be evidenced in a thought experiment by René Descartes. It attempts to show a clear and understandable indication that we are not merely body; in fact, that the soul can be understood best without the body. Imagine that you do not have a body. You are not merely invisible, as if you had slipped on an enchanted ring from *The Lord of the Rings*. You are in front of a mirror but nothing is actually there; no face to wash, no hair to comb, no teeth to brush. The very conceivability of this scenario, some think, shows that it is possible. And if it is even possible to imagine yourself without a body, this shows that the soul and body are distinct things. We cannot, for example, conceive of eating without teeth and a stomach, so eating is not something that can be achieved without the body. But we can conceive of existing without a body, so this shows an important distinction between soul and body.

The argument above as well as Plato's, along with appeals to immortality in general, proceed on a real separation of the soul from the body. In themselves these arguments show only that the soul is different, not immortal. What needs to be added to this chain of thought is the corruptibility inherent in the body. If the body, as a composite of different material substances, necessarily will perish when those substances one day come apart, then the simplicity and indivisibility of the soul, we can imagine, will protect it from this same perishable fate, ensuring a life beyond the material.

Can you conceive of yourself standing in front of a mirror without a body?

23

Truth and Falsehood

The liar has a problem with the truth. It is not that he does not know the truth. Perhaps we can say the liar knows the truth all too well so that he can conceal it with his own words. Truth, it seems, is a part of the human world and it has a hold on us in every facet of life; even the dishonest seem to have a hold on it, so that they can distort it to their own ends.

But what is true, and if we step beyond what is true to something even higher, what is truth? Truth does not just concern the realms of rigorous enquiry such as science and logic. Truth is something which permeates our social interactions, our thought, and our relation to reality at the deepest levels.

STATEMENTS AND THE TRUTH

Perhaps we can start by looking at some rather simple statements. The sun is a star. Three added to three is six. We would never think that these statements are false. They are true. But now comes the difficult part: what does it mean to be true or false? There are many ways to look at this question. We can consider the statement "the sun is a star" merely as a linguistic statement or we can view it as a representation of a state of affairs, how things are in reality. We can also think of truth as telling us about the world, truth as a part of reality, or merely as some kind of convention we use to communicate meaning.

In looking at truth, the first thing we should consider is whether all or only some things can be true or false. In doing so, we direct our attention to whether a statement is capable of being true or false. To be true or false, a statement must be making a claim. The phrase "cheese is disgusting" is neither true nor false, because it is the mere opinion of an individual. Likewise, prayers and commands, to add a few other categories of non-statements, do not claim anything and so cannot be true or false.

How do we prove that the statement "the Moon has many craters and they all have Latin names" is true?

THE CORRESPONDENCE THEORY OF TRUTH

One of the most common theories of truth is the *correspondence theory* of truth, which has a very practical appeal. In this theory a statement can be declared true if reality as it actually is corresponds to the statement being made of it. The focus of this theory is on reality, not on the proposition or statement which does (or does not) correspond to it. So although reality and a statement (if it is true) do correspond to each other, the reason is that a statement corresponds to reality, in the sense of being checked against reality, like a test compared to an answer key. If it turns out that there is no tooth fairy, then the statement "there is a tooth fairy" is false for this very reason. This is a rather simple statement, and so basically involves only one factor, the tooth fairy itself. For more complicated statements, such as "the Moon has many craters and they all have Latin names," we have to see whether the Moon has many craters and if all the craters have Latin names. If the Moon is full of Latin-named craters, then the statement is true.

In these examples we may distinguish in the correspondence theory two elements that have a necessarily close relationship. One we may call

Correspondence Theory

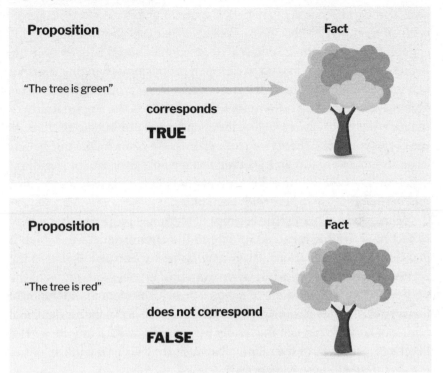

the *proposition*, while the other is the *fact*. The *fact* is how reality actually is, while the *proposition*, as a linguistic expression, does or does not align with the fact of the matter and is accordingly true or false.

Since there is an acknowledged heavy dependence of propositions on the facts, some philosophers have gone farther than the correspondence theory and adhered to an identity theory of truth. The *identity theory*, as the name implies, claims that a proposition is no different than its fact, if the proposition is true. In this framework, truth properly belongs to the proposition in a fundamental way.

THE COHERENCE THEORY OF TRUTH

The *coherence theory* of truth is another competitor for the proper account of truth and falsity. In this theory something is true if it fits together into a coherent system with other beliefs held in the system. One unique feature of this kind of system is that it does not make this appeal to truth by something outside of the belief system, as is the case with the correspondence theory, where the truth must accord with the facts. There is no need for independent justification in the coherence theory: it is sufficient that each and every belief, something asserted as true, agrees with all the other beliefs in the system. What this shows is that in the coherentist system there is no real distinction between belief and truth. In fact it is belief, understood as different propositions hanging together in a unified fashion, which determines that these propositions are true. One reason attracting adherents to this theory is the impossibility of seeing what reality is really like independent of our beliefs about it, as the correspondence theory of truth claims. We cannot take our beliefs in one hand and reality in the other and see how they are the same and different. The best we can expect is that our beliefs agree with each other, and in the best case cohere with each other.

More recent work on the concept of truth has proposed that it may in fact be a flexible term, adaptable to the circumstances in which it is used. In some situations, truth may be best construed as it is in the correspondence theory while approximating in other situations to the understanding offered by the coherentist theory. The mere consideration of this type of pluralist account gives rise to a question about the fundamental nature of truth. What is it that really determines truth, if anything? Is it language, or reality, or the relation between the two, or is truth an entity transcending all these categories?

Coherence Theory

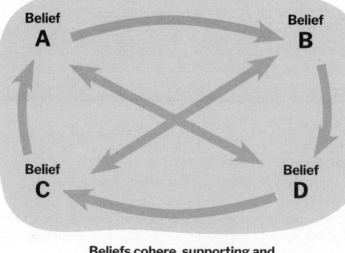

Beliefs cohere, supporting and enforcing each other.

24

Nietzsche's Superman

The Superman is an idea found in Friedrich Nietzsche (1844–1900)'s book *Thus Spoke Zarathustra*. Despite the coincidence, Nietzsche's figure had nothing to do with the superhero of the same name. Nietzsche's original term was *Übermensch*, which can be translated as Overman or Superman.

The theory behind the Superman has proved to be variously interpreted and controversial, most notably in its appropriation by the Nazis as a symbol fitting for the Master Race.

THE FALL OF CHRISTIANITY AND THE NEED FOR A SUBSTITUTE

Nietzsche famously proclaimed that God is dead. This was not a claim that the Creator had suddenly keeled over on his heavenly throne. It was a claim about the collapse of belief in Christianity, and along with this collapse the radical changes in morality sweeping across Europe in Nietzsche's own day. In his mind, the time and place had come for God to be replaced by something above him, the idea of the Superman.

Thus Spoke Zarathustra is told as a story, and for that reason can be difficult to understand, as is true of the fascinating but often riddling way in which the characters speak. The main figure in the book is Zarathustra, or Zoroaster, the founder of the ancient and now obscure religion of Zoroastrianism. The book is meant to be at once literature and philosophy, communicating Nietzsche's ideas in a powerful narrative form.

Although Nietzsche's idea that God was dead was a description of what he was observing at the time, this does not mean he did not have an opinion on the demise of Christianity. In fact, he delighted in the fall of the old religion, for he saw in it a weakness and believed it to be an obstacle to the creation of something better, the arrival of his Superman. From his perspective, Christianity elevated the plight of the weak and the pitiful, at the expense of life-affirming values. In particular,

Friedrich Nietzsche advocated for a Superman to take over the notion of God as an ethical guidepost.

Nietzsche thought that Christianity devalued the present life in two ways, by focusing on the afterlife instead of our current circumstances and by holding up chastity as a virtue. He argued that this negative view of sex interferes with and wrongfully tries to stamp out the reproduction impulse vital for life.

THE SUPERMAN AND POWER

The Superman was an idea that was supposed to answer the need for a new type of morality, a man with the capacity to surpass not only the old belief in God, but also the limitations of the human race as it had as yet existed. There is a poetic way in which we are no longer obligated to follow God since he has perished, but we are to follow the guidance of nature, which is represented by the Earth. Nature has granted to us certain impulses and capacities, which we are to fulfil. The overriding concern of the Superman is power, a term with broad application for Nietzsche. Power is defined as what is good, and so weakness is bad. Nietzsche also thought that the feeling of power was as important as power itself. This reaching out for power has come to be known as the *will to power*. The will to power should not be primarily understood as an attempt to subdue other people under one's dominion, though it could have this kind of application as well. The main function of the will to power is the drive to create and fashion yourself in the way you desire. The very nature of the concept seems to preclude a detailed account of what Nietzsche meant by will to power, but his statement that man "seeks to discharge his power" captures the scope of the sentiment very well. A desire to develop and express ourselves, which differs from person to person, can be seen in all of us.

THE SUPERMAN COMPARED TO MERE HUMANS

Some of the rhetoric used by Nietzsche to tie his conception of the Superman to the natural order is that humankind is scarcely valuable in itself, comparing it to a worm. Humans are little more than apes, he

Important Terms

Death of God
The demise of Christianity and, along with it, its form of morality.

Herd mentality
The way in which most people unreflectively adopt the thoughts and practices of their own culture.

Will to power
The way in which each person seeks to get a hold of power in order to personally develop, to "discharge our energies."

claims, and the real value in humans consists in being transitional to the Superman. The Superman is in a unique position to advance not merely his own causes but that of the human race as a whole. The mass of humanity is unable to change the course of history for the better the way the Superman can. This is because the common people display a herd mentality.

Most people lack an individual will to remake the world for the better and just unreflectively follow along with what they have been taught and adhere to the practices of their given society.

WHAT DOES THE SUPERMAN LOOK LIKE?

Someone who is a Superman is able to affect the world through his vision and values in a radical way. One favorite example of Nietzsche was Napoleon, who affected the life of Europe for centuries to come in its political, legal, and even ethical order of life. In some ways Nietzsche fixates on the mere fact that Napoleon brought about a radical change in human order more than on the details of this change or the means

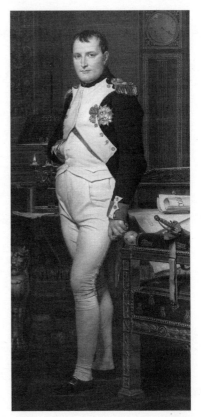

Napoleon is a good example of a Superman, someone who flouts convention and blazes a new trail.

by which he brought it about—broadscale war. You could say Nietzsche was indifferent to this, caring only that Napoleon created a new world, regardless of what it was like. The Superman is someone who directs his will to power to overcome the troubles and problems of this world, at least as he sees them.

SUPERMAN VS CHRISTIANITY

Since the Superman is a trailblazer, and since Nietzsche is assuming (at least in his context) that God may be dead but Christianity is not, the Superman must set himself against the morality and practices which Christianity upholds. So at the same time as the Superman seeks his new world, it is to be built upon the razed foundations of the old world. In the end what the Superman needs to overcome is this system of values, to cross over the "bridge" of mankind as it currently is to a new vision. When the old order has been demolished, humans will be directionless and in need of the guidance only the Superman can provide.

Mankind is a "bridge" to the concept of the Superman

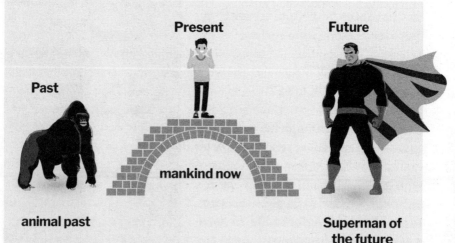

Past

Present

Future

animal past

mankind now

Superman of
the future

25

Kierkegaard's Three Stages on Life's Way

Søren Kierkegaard (1813–55) lived a short but intensely passionate life. He is familiar as a name to many, but the content of his philosophy is often unknown except for the vague associations he has to Existentialism. Part of his neglect owes to the fact that he wrote in Danish, a language with relatively few speakers. Nevertheless in the last hundred years he has earned a worldwide reputation as a philosopher of the highest merit.

THE THREE STAGES

Above all, Kierkegaard was a practical philosopher, focusing on the difficulties of day-to-day life. In this chapter we will explore his three stages on life's way: the esthetic, ethical, and religious lives. Before we look at the particular meanings of these lives, it is helpful to talk first about their relationship to each other. These three stages are by no means exclusive. It is possible to live a partly esthetic and a partly religious life, for example. In the ideal case, a person ought to advance ultimately to the religious life. This optimal condition often does not come about, however, and instead you are stuck living an esthetic or ethical life. Advancement comes about through personal reflection, and not merely by becoming older. Thus advancement is not guaranteed; it must come about through a spiritual transformation. Both the esthetic and the ethical life fall short of the richness and meaning of the religious life.

THE ESTHETIC LIFE

The esthetic life is a life of sensation. Its characteristic feature is one of immediacy. People who live like this fail to turn and analyze their

Søren Kierkegaard has been influential as a writer, theologian, and philosopher.

lives with the aim of improvement. This should not be surprising, as the esthete lives only in the now and gives no consideration for his future. Kierkegaard thought that most people live their lives this way. He also lived this way at one time, eating fine food and hiring coaches to take him on leisurely strolls for mere enjoyment. The immediacy and impermanence marking the esthete express themselves through pleasure. This not only condemns the esthetic person to a shallow life but in a more fundamental way prohibits them from giving real focus and consistency to their lives.

We can even mark a distinction between unrefined and refined esthetes. The unrefined, of course, cannot help but indulge in all manner of immediacy and pleasure. The refined esthete may find a higher level of pleasure, such as in philosophy, literature, and the arts. Nevertheless, at bottom it is a disordered life lacking a greater cohesion. What binds the different kinds of esthetes together is that life is something done to them. Because of their focus on transient pleasure, they experience life as a series of fortunes and misfortunes—responsibility and agency do not even enter the picture.

The heart of the esthete's problems lies in finding himself at odds with himself since the objects of his interest and energy are so superficial that he cannot be satisfied. One tactic he may employ to delude himself is the *rotation method*: he flits from one pleasure to the next, often enjoying them in some novel or peculiar way, hoping that a different experience

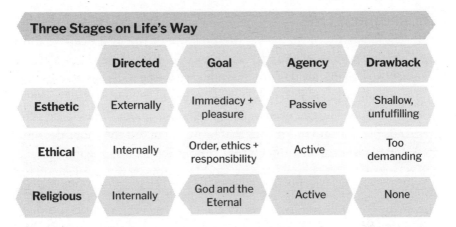

Three Stages on Life's Way				
	Directed	Goal	Agency	Drawback
Esthetic	Externally	Immediacy + pleasure	Passive	Shallow, unfulfilling
Ethical	Internally	Order, ethics + responsibility	Active	Too demanding
Religious	Internally	God and the Eternal	Active	None

of the same old way of life will deliver a more satisfying experience. He takes a cooking class but then never cooks for himself again, or buys a book but reads only the last chapter, or falls in love but inevitably becomes bored with his lover.

THE ETHICAL LIFE

Only when someone has seen through the shallowness of the esthetic way of life does he detach himself from it, becoming now prepared for the ethical form of life. This is defined almost by direct contrast with the esthetic. Whereas the esthetic life is consumed with the outer world, the ethical life is focused on the inner self. The ethical life confers an outlook of order that the esthetic life completely lacks. There is a semi-religious aspect to this change from the esthetic to the ethical, which Kierkegaard dubs repentance. Because the ethical man is oriented toward himself and not the outer world, it does not bother him if he fails in some worldly sense. Instead his life is gauged by the honest effort and commitment he applies to the task. In sum, the ethical life is committed to the development of one's abilities and the assumption of responsibility, such as marriage and family life.

Among the difficulties of the ethical life is that its demands are too high. Anyone who pursues an ethical life will feel, and rightfully so, inept at keeping the demands of such a life. Even more troubling to Kierkegaard, when a person is given over to the ethical life completely, he loses his sense of self within the smothering universality of the values to which he has subjected himself. The mismatch between the life he aspires to and the life he can actually attain leads the ethical man to despair. If the despair has the right effect, it will lead to the religious way of life.

THE RELIGIOUS LIFE

The religious way of life views the purpose of life as a deep relation between the individual will and God's will. For Kierkegaard, Abraham is the prototype of this kind of life. The ethical life with its focus on morality and reason is superseded in the religious life as the individual submits his will to God. The orientation of the religious man acknowledges the demands of God, and this means that he must make a conscious decision to order his life toward the eternal. In particular this means seeking the relationship made possible by God becoming a man in Jesus. This involves a "leap of faith" because man cannot fully understand the paradox of God becoming man. In the end, the religious person does not entirely give up the world of the esthetic and ethical outlooks, but accords them their rightful place, which limits their value in light of the eternal. Everything in the end must be submitted to the eternal.

The Rotation Method

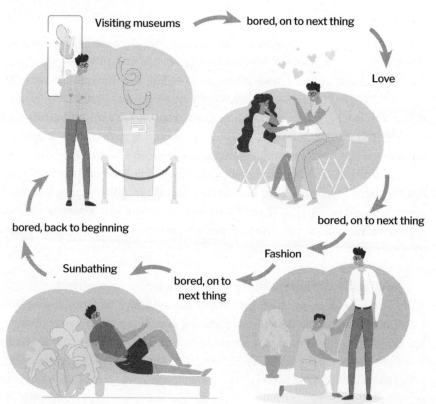

Visiting museums → bored, on to next thing

Love

bored, on to next thing

Fashion

bored, on to next thing

Sunbathing

bored, back to beginning

26

Acting for the Greatest Utility

There is a sense in which we all act for utility at one time or another, in the sense of trying to maximize a certain feature which we hold to be of value. We may try to maximize the money we make by being careful how we spend it, or our weekly time so that our schedules fit as many useful activities as possible.

There is also a broader sense in which we can approach the entirety of life with the same goal in mind, maximizing utility as an ethical theory. Utilitarianism, a philosophy of maximizing the good, has precisely this aim in mind. Though formally articulated fairly recently, in the 1900s, it's an idea that can nevertheless claim to have ancient pedigree, as the Ancient Epicureans did indeed seek to maximize the good, with an understanding that the good to be pursued was simply whatever brought about pleasure. Modern conceptions of utilitarianism, as we will see, also tie together notions of pleasure with the good, while extending their consideration of the good beyond the self. It is not just maximization of the good for oneself: an aim of utilitarianism is to maximize the good of all, or nearly all, people.

A PRACTICAL THEORY

As we might expect from an ethical theory, the practical aspect of utilitarianism comes into play when it guides conduct. Yet, although other ethical ideals may be liable to the criticism that they are too abstract and general to be of any use, the upside of utilitarianism is that one can at least in theory derive a specific answer to a specific question by discovering the total good expected to come out of alternative possibilities.

Right action does not come from:	Right action does come from:
Rules	Maximization of good, understood as human pleasure or happiness
Laws	
Duties	
Virtues	

What makes an action right when considered in the light of utilitarianism? Which criterion is used to assess the different possibilities for how to act? To answer this, we must examine the way in which utilitarianism, as a theory, relevantly takes facts and conditions into account. Only when these facts and conditions are taken into account in the right way can it be known whether a given action is correct. As mentioned, utilitarianism is an egalitarian philosophy, treating as equal the concerns of each human. The scope of relevance also extends to consequences in a broader sense. For example, if we decide to treat

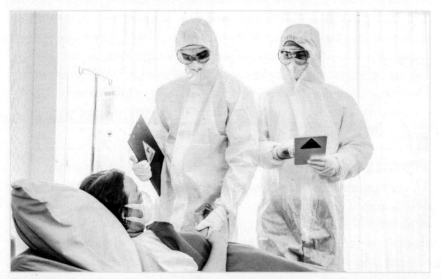

Patients may be kept in quarantine if they have a contagious illness even though it makes them worse off, as it maximizes the well-being of the community as a whole.

severely ill but also highly contagious patients in a hospital, we should ask not only how this will affect those who are being treated, but also how it will affect the other patients in the hospital, the medical personnel, and staff, as well as the broader community in which the hospital is situated. So the impacts of a given action must be taken into account as it brings about its effects, in the most expansive meaning of that term.

WHAT SHOULD BE MAXIMIZED?

However, looking at things from this broader perspective will not tell us what to do, for we still have to fill out our notion of what we are trying to maximize in the world. There are different schools of thought among utilitarians as to what good, or utility, we ought to pursue. For some we are to look at a greater sum, all things considered, of the good, which is defined as well-being. Well-being itself can be defined in different ways. It can have a subjective component, such as maximizing pleasure or minimizing suffering. If we are to develop this idea further, pursuing the idea that well-being is pleasure, we then have to pursue a calculus of every person's total pleasure and their total non-pleasure, including pain,

Jeremy Bentham was one of the fathers of utilitarianism.

sufferings, and loss, all of which relevantly affect pleasure. Returning to the example given, we notionally add up the pleasure of the patients being admitted into the hospital, as well as any non-pleasures they will incur, and we extend this procedure to everyone who could be affected by these contagious patients. Likewise we perform the same mental procedure if we take the route of not admitting these patients. What would be the "cost" of admitting these patients, in terms of pleasure and non-pleasure? Whatever total sum of pleasures, minus the non-pleasures, outweighs all other options is what we ought to choose and act upon. Not only will it be right to act in whatever way the scales tip in favor of this pleasure calculus, it will be incorrect and indeed morally wrong to act in any other way.

IS SEEKING UTILITY TOO DIFFICULT TO DETERMINE?
It should be evident that acting with utility in mind, precisely because of this adding up of a correct course of action, is at odds with other theories of ethical behavior, such as those which put weight upon our duties or appeal to principles other than utility. Because of the time-consuming nature of determining the right course of action, Jeremy Bentham (1748–1832), often considered the father of utilitarianism, advocated that for efficiency it is sometimes impractical to gather all information relevant for a decision. In such conditions, one must simply make the utilitarian choice based on what one does know.

CLASSICAL AND RULE UTILITARIANISM
There are some important variations concerning utilitarian principles. Classical Utilitarianism or Act Utilitarianism has been described above, since it offers guidance on deciding on a particular act. Rule Utilitarianism, by contrast, does not descend to the level of each particular act, but rather advocates that the rightness of an action is in conformity with a rule formulated to maximize utility in general circumstances. Thus

Two Types of Utilitarianism

Classical Utilitarianism	Rule Utilitarianism
Act in such a way as to maximize utility	Act in such a way as if it were a general rule, a particular course of action would then maximize utility

in principle, it is more than possible that a given rule, generated for general application, might in a particular instance actually reduce utility, although in the long run and in most instances it would increase utility.

Despite a reputation as a cold, calculated, and dispassionate arbiter of action, utilitarianism as a philosophical belief has often been characterized by its proponents as the maximization of happiness. For in the end, it is happiness that is in view. Utility just gets us there faster.

27
Acting in Line with Duty

You hear a knock at the door, and you open it to find the secret police. They wish to know the location of some dissidents, whom you know to be good and innocent people. You happen to know where these fugitives are—in your dining room. You could tell the police you have never heard of these fugitives and they will promptly leave you alone. Instead, you tell the police you do know where they are, and point out that the fugitives are in your living room.

KANT AND THE ABSOLUTE NATURE OF DUTY

The above story accurately, if shockingly, conveys the views of Immanuel Kant (1724–1804) and the absolute nature of his *deontological ethics*. Deontological ethics comprise an ethical theory where duty (Greek *deon*) makes a claim as to what we are supposed to do. Turning in fugitives in the hypothetical story above was, in fact, explicitly endorsed by Kant for he believed that one of his duties was not to lie. This duty extended to all times and all circumstances. The fact that the police will take away the dissidents to some undesirable fate is secondary to the importance of faithful duty.

It will be apparent that deontological ethics is not a consequentialist ethical theory. It does not first look to calculate the costs or benefits, good or bad, of a given course of action, and then decide whether to act based on some tabulation of ethical scores. There is a strong emphasis on the moral agent's relation to the world.

PERSONHOOD AND DEONTOLOGY

Kant's ethics center on the concept of personhood. Personhood, not found outside the human race, is in turn defined by the ability to use reason, which people possess simply by being human. This notion of the person is in some sense sacrosanct, in that we are not to treat people as

Immanuel Kant is known for the rigidity and consistency of his morals and his philosophical systems.

other than persons. This means we are to use people not as objects but as subjects, capable of reason in their own right. This respect for the subject, regardless of concern for our own pleasure, happiness, or consequences, can also be described as a totalizing adherence to the law itself. Of course, this observance of duty has what we may call a good and a bad side. On one side, as in the example of the secret police, deontology is considered too strident and unyielding, unable to accommodate the complexities of everyday moral life with its call to absolute obedience. On the other side, deontology is able to provide a clear and consistent path of action in many cases, even if adhering to it may be hard.

THE CATEGORICAL IMPERATIVE
Kant's formulation of what he called the categorical imperative is intimately tied in with his whole system of deontological ethics. The categorical

Categorical Imperative

Treat every person as a rational subject, not an object

Act only in such a way as you would wish to be a universal law

imperative is a maxim or rule whose adherence is required merely by virtue of being a human. The existence of this formulation shows that for Kant, and for most forms of deontology in general, the particular forms of duty demanded of us are not ours to choose. Deontology is a not a build-your-own-rules theory but claims to derive its mandates from an ethical order of how human life should be led. This accounts for the universal nature of deontology, its applicability to all humans, as well as its rationality—a logical formalization of ethical demands that other humans, because they are rational, are also capable of following and understanding. Kant believed, in one of the many formulations of the categorical imperative, that we should act only in such a way that we would wish for that act to be generalized into a universal law. What this universalization amounts to is not only that it has wide applicability but moreover that it is universal for every rational agent. For example, you would not want "lie when it is convenient" to become a universal moral law, so you should not lie in the particular case of being asked by the secret police where the innocent fugitives are hiding, even if it is tempting.

AGENT-CENTERED AND VICTIM-CENTERED DEONTOLOGY

There are two aspects of deontological ethics which can be conceived of as complementary, the *agent-centered* and the *victim-centered*. The agent-centered is the more positive characterization, positing certain obligations that are incumbent upon agents. The patient-centered view shifts the focus to those who would be adversely affected if duties are not properly followed. This is a negative characterization in that it emphasizes what ought not to be done to others in terms of the rights they possess. Another formulation of the categorical imperative focuses on human agency and rationality. From this vantage point, we should never treat people as merely ends but as ends in themselves. This is an acknowledgement that other people are rational moral agents.

Four Divisions of Duties

Perfect duty to oneself Example: do not commit suicide	Perfect duty to others Example: do not make unkeepable promises
Imperfect duty to oneself Example: develop your talents	Imperfect duty to others Example: advance others' happiness

PERFECT AND IMPERFECT DUTIES

Kant divided deontological ethics into four areas: perfect duties to oneself, imperfect duties to oneself, perfect duties to others, and imperfect duties to others. The major distinctive feature of a perfect duty is that it always applies. One must always follow the dictates of a perfect duty. An imperfect duty allows for some measure of freedom. That is, although it must be followed, it can be fulfilled in different ways, and at different times, at the discretion of someone who is trying to fulfill this imperfect duty.

Kant gave examples of each of these four kinds of duty. Not committing suicide is a perfect duty to oneself. Not making unkeepable promises to others is a perfect duty to others. To develop your own talents is an imperfect duty to yourself; contributing to the happiness of others is an imperfect duty to others. These imperfect duties of self-development and helping others to achieve happiness allow for differences in their pursuit and fulfillment. So one need not give up every spare waking minute to serve in a soup kitchen, since the where, when, how much, and how often of helping others is largely up to us. Choosing to help others live a happy life is a moral demand, but the details of how we live this out are determined by our own lives and goals.

For Kant the moral world we live in is a world dependent to a large degree, if not exclusively, on our relationships to other humans, rational agents with whom we share a network of ethical obligations and ethical goals.

Would you tell the truth if police demanded to know where innocent prisoners were, and you knew where they were?

28

Acting in Accordance with Virtue

Would you like to be happy as well as virtuous? Would you like to be formed and shaped into a certain kind of person? Virtue ethics is an ethical theory emphasizing the development of the person as an ethical agent. For this reason virtue ethics is sometimes referred to as an agent-centered rather than an action-centered system of ethics.

This does not mean that virtue ethics has nothing to do with actions, since any system of ethics must prescribe a course of actions. Rather the shift of focus to the agent, the person who acts, is an acknowledgement that when it comes to actions what we are primarily concerned about is the character of an individual.

ARISTOTLE AND HAPPINESS

Virtue ethics begins with Aristotle (384–322 BCE), and extends to the current day, with many philosophical proponents advocating for a neo-Aristotelian adaptation of Aristotle's original ideas. To start with Aristotle is to see from his perspective what the purpose of life is. Without going into too many details, Aristotle was committed to the thought that happiness is what people pursue while living their lives. Virtue ethics, in line with this, seeks to achieve happiness, a more robust notion than the modern understanding which reduces it to a pleasant, transitory emotion. In contrast, happiness for Aristotle is something achieved, if not experienced, over the course of a lifetime, and comes about within the enacted practice of wisdom and virtue.

THE UNION OF VIRTUE AND HAPPINESS

If virtue ethics focuses on what kind of people we ought to be, then how do we become those people? Virtue ethics places attention, unsurprisingly, on virtue. Virtue is primarily seen in, and characteristic of, a virtuous person. This does not mean that the virtuous person is incapable of acting incorrectly. It is more than possible for a virtuous person to fail to act correctly on a given occasion, but it is characteristic of him not to act viciously—that is, without virtue. To act virtuously is the type of life typified in a virtuous person.

TWO KINDS OF VIRTUE

Virtue itself consists of two kinds. There are the intellectual virtues and the ethical or moral virtues. In another broad division, the intellectual virtues are broken up into those which concern theoretical reasoning and the kind of thinking associated with actions. The list of ethical virtues is probably very similar to one you might have: courage, temperance or self-control, liberality, magnificence, honor, equanimity, truthfulness, friendship, and justice. Aristotle has other virtues, such as wit, which many today would think desirable but not a virtue, while he leaves out traits of character numbered among the virtues today, such as self-awareness, forgiveness, or even traditionally religious virtues such as charity or hope.

THE GOLDEN MEAN

An act is virtuous when it hits what Aristotle calls the "golden mean" between two extremes. To take what is probably the clearest of examples, courage, we say that courage is avoiding both brashness and cowardice.

Virtues

Intellectual

Moral

Theoretical

Practical (concerned with action)

The "Golden Mean"

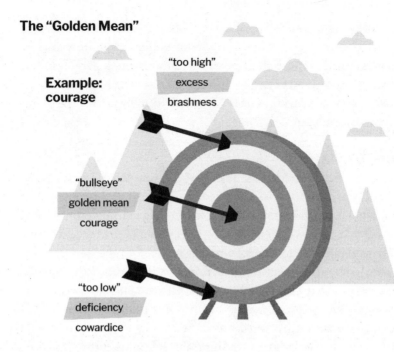

Being brash or too bold is an extreme of excess while cowardice is an extreme of deficiency. Another clear example is liberality, concerned with procuring and spending money. Its excess is prodigality or being a spendthrift, while the deficiency of liberality is illiberality or stinginess. Insofar as there are two wrong paths to virtue, both are extremes, each extreme failing to be virtuous and being said to "miss the mark" of virtue.

VIRTUE AS A STATE OF CHARACTER

Just as virtue lies in hitting the mark between two extremes, as is appropriate to any given virtue, Aristotle thinks that possessing virtue means to possess it as a state. The fact that virtue is a state once again brings attention to the fact that virtue ethics is concerned with the character of an individual and not so much individual actions. That is, despite popular conceptions, you are not brave, in Aristotle's conception, if you perform one outstanding act of bravery. You must be characteristically brave to have bravery as a virtue. Thus conceived, this state of bravery is part of character.

Yet, if we wish to understand the relationship between virtue and action more fully, we have to see how they are closely related. One action does not make an individual virtuous; only the slow and deliberate accumulation of acting virtuously over time can achieve this state of character. When an individual has been habituated into this state of character, then they are virtuous. At this point, virtue has become a kind of second nature for the person, and the kind of actions they will perform necessarily will be virtuous, for the very reason that someone with a virtuous character will act virtuously.

PRACTICAL WISDOM

All this talk about aiming at, and perhaps sometimes missing, the virtue between two extremes raises the question of how the mean of virtue

Aristotle associated virtue with happiness, and thought virtue had both moral and intellectual components.

is ever achieved. Intimately related to this question is Aristotle's concept of *phronesis,* understood in English to be "practical wisdom." Practical wisdom is not something that comes about easily or quickly. Rather, it is achieved with the experience of age. So part of achieving practical wisdom is the process of maturation in life. But since life must be lived before such an acquisition, namely the period of education in youth, it is during this period that the process of habituation in the virtues occurs. Only when the virtues have been instilled in someone in the form of character, and he combines this with practical wisdom, can it be said that this man is virtuous. In the concept of practical reason, we see that anyone who lacks this ability will in particular cases lack the insight to act in a virtuous way, and more broadly, will be incapable of acting virtuously as a characteristic expression of who he is as a person.

To summarize: virtue ethics, as expressed by Aristotle, maintains that the ultimate end of human activity is happiness. The path to achieving this is by leading a life that is characterized by virtue over a whole lifetime, virtue being defined intellectually and morally as the mean between extremes of excess and deficiency.

29

Artistic Judgment and Value

The value and appreciation of art, especially particular works of art, varies widely and with differing degrees of enthusiasm from person to person. These differing tastes can be the occasion for serious disagreement, an apparent refusal to concede that other people have different and equally legitimate tastes, that "beauty is (only) in the eye of the beholder."

We say that we love Shakespeare, while someone else shares that reading his plays was the worst part of her education. A friend says that he thinks the newest superhero movie is great, while you will do anything to avoid subjecting yourself to such puerile cinema. On and on we could go, and all the while we have a conception, hidden even from ourselves, that there is some standard, or principle, or framework in which artwork can be understood to explain its beauty and wonder. But what reasons can we possibly give for what art is, what good art is, and what is beautiful, good, and true in art? To approach art, we will look at esthetics. This is the branch of philosophy that deals with art, often more narrowly confined to the beautiful in art. Esthetics derives from the Greek word *aisthesis* (sensation) and refers to the primary role which sight and hearing play in our appreciation of art. Because of the importance of beauty in esthetics, and since beauty is not confined to art, beauty sometimes will also require attention to nature or other areas outside of art.

KANT: BEAUTY IS NOT RATIONAL
Immanuel Kant (1724–1804), perhaps surprisingly given the central place of reason found in his other works, conceived of esthetics as something distinct from reason. A central aspect of his theory is that in

the appreciation of beauty the mind is in "free play." His view centers on the role of concepts, and when we see beauty for what it is, our imagination is not hindered by concepts. What does it mean for a concept to hinder the imagination? When we apply a concept, however broad or narrow the concept, it creates a particular view of the object to which we apply it, and it prevents the freedom we experience in actual experiences of beauty. What exactly Kant has in mind, considered from the experiential perspective of the first person, is in dispute. But at least one aim of admitting a role for imagination

Are the works of Shakespeare beautiful or not?

in our perception of beauty is the pleasure we feel as we experience it. Kant also believed that there was a sense in which beauty is objective. This means that, as an object of beauty, the object is as available to you as it is to me (at least theoretically), since we are both in possession of a common human faculty which perceives beauty.

HOW DO WE PERCEIVE BEAUTY?

Kant's view on beauty is admittedly vague, but serves as a good segue to several distinctions, and so sources of dispute, within the field of esthetic thinking. One is whether beauty is something that is perceived by our senses, or if it is instead comprehended by our rational faculty. Kant's view above conceives of beauty as something taken in through non-rational avenues, and this in fact explains why he describes the process in a way that defies formulation into hard and fast rules or principles. Some theorists construe beauty in a formal sense, a commitment to the idea that there are regularities, or a canon, to which art conforms. Others think that art is a matter of taste, but this does not necessarily commit them to the belief that all art is relative to a perceiver.

ABSTRACT AND REPRESENTATIONAL ART

Another major distinction in esthetics is not the way in which an observer sees, but in the very object of art itself. This is the distinction between abstract and representational art. Whereas representational art attempts

Artistic Judgment

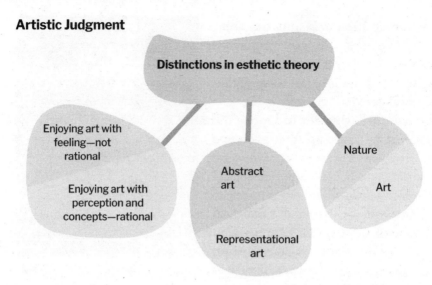

to depict some feature of the world—such as a flower, landscape, or a person or event—with some degree of fidelity to what it is representing, abstract art makes no claim to represent in this literal way. Instead it may take a form wholly alien to the subject in front of the artist, if indeed there is a subject at all.

THE FORMAL ELEMENTS OF ART

This distinction between abstract and representational art, which is defined on the basis of the object of art under consideration, brings into focus the formal properties of art. This is to say, art understood insofar as it offers itself as something to be available as seen or heard. *Form* in this sense is meant to be whatever structure accounts for the beauty of the work. So the beauty seen in Da Vinci's *Mona Lisa* in terms of form could be considered as the use of a high landscape perspective, the asymmetry of the right and left sides, the masterly employment of *sfumato* in the gradations of color, and the soft contours of Mona Lisa herself in contrast to the harsh lines of the countryside depicted behind her. A more rigorous treatment might delve into mathematical or geometrical relations among the different objects in the painting.

It is easy to understand the appeal of an authoritative standard for beauty such as formalism. Beauty is a precious entity and encounters with it are rare and often fleeting. In the search for an undeniable core of beauty, we like to think that we can possess it with more permanence than beauty itself allows. It was at one time a common assumption that there was no need to search for its source; beauty sprang from nature, and art arose as an imitation of nature. As art criticism reached its maturity in the 1800s, and up to the present day, more and more emphasis has been laid on art as the source of beauty, or as at least the focal point of interest. Beauty, whatever it is, must be sought between the gaps and the commonalities of nature and art.

What formal aspects could we appeal to in saying that the Mona Lisa *is beautiful?*

30
The Philosophy of Time

It is easy to take time for granted. Not in the way we make use of it, letting the finite amount of time we are given slip away unnoticed. But rather we think of time as something so familiar and known that we do not recognize how highly dependent our experience of it is on how we conceive of it.

If you have a clock or watch with a round face, hour and minute hands, you may think of time as circular in some way. Or take for instance another common way of conceptualizing time as an arrow or even just a line moving from left to right. The left is the past, the middle is the present and the right is the future. You may think that this is just a common-sense representation of time. But not all societies conceive of time in this way. For instance, the Ancient Greeks conceived of the future as behind and the past as in front, on the grounds that what is yet to come is hidden from us and so behind us, while the past is open to our inspection and so in front of our eyes.

THE A-THEORY AND B-THEORY OF TIME

The above shows that our understanding of time is strongly influenced by how we are able to think of it. Sometimes it is impossible to think of time outside these familiar aids to illustration. This will help us as we discuss what have come to be called the *A-theory* and *B-theory* of time, competing accounts of how we understand time. The normal mode of understanding time, which we may call the unreflective and common approach, is to understand time as consisting of past, present, and future. This theory of time is called the A-theory. The more modern theory, in favor with most scientists and philosophers of time, is the B-theory. This theory orders time in a relative sequence, by which some events or things come prior and others come later.

This is the most common division of theories of time, though within

A common representation of time's progress

past   present   future

both of these views there are further distinctions, which we will also consider. Far from only being speculative affairs, these theories are important for many diverse areas of human life. They affect our view of ourselves and our relation to the world, our notions of change, cause and effect, ageing, and even the reality of time itself.

From a broader perspective A-theory appeals to an objective understanding of time, while B-theory is relative. This distinction is clarified when we see that in the A-theory of time the present is given a privileged position while the B-theory denies a singular importance to what is happening at the moment. In the A-theory the "past" is defined as such in relation to the present, the "future" is defined in relation to the present, and the present enjoys its privilege because it is the time occurring now, at this moment, as you read. The B-theory does not center and privilege any time as an A-theorist does with the present. In B-theory all times are equal, even if the sequence requires that some times come before or after other times. In a moment we will see how B-theorists make sense of what we call the present.

A-THEORY: THE MOVING SPOTLIGHT AND
GROWING BLOCK THEORY

Among A-theorists there is a diversity of viewpoints as to what time is, and we will now look at several of these opinions. We began by noting how we as humans conceptualize time in different ways and how this informs our understanding of its nature. The following variations on the A-theory of time creatively illustrate our dependence on metaphor in pinning down some notion of time. The *Moving Spotlight* theory of time is just what it sounds like. The uniqueness of the present is accounted for by comparison to a moving spotlight drawing attention, and importance, to what is currently happening.

This image nicely shows the special nature of the present in contrast to past and future, but also conveys the acknowledgement that the future

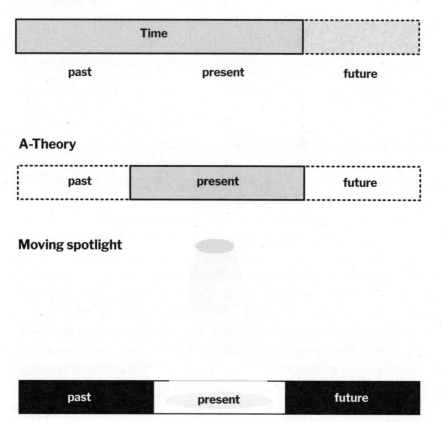

and past are real in some sense, but are, in keeping with the metaphor, off-stage waiting in the wings. Past and future thus exist, but they are not foregrounded in the way the present is. Another view is the *Growing Block* view of time. On this view time "grows," or comes to be as the universe grows. Thus the past comes to be the present, and the universe grows, so that it is larger than before. The future, not yet existing, will also become part of the present, and when it does so, it will become a part of the growing block as well, at which point the universe will be even larger than it is now. Because of its insistence on the reality of the present in the growing block, there is a denial that the future exists in any robust sense. That is to say, the present does not come before the future, because if the future existed right now, it would be a part of the growing block already, but it clearly is not.

B-theory

Only when each "frame" of time is combined do we have a proper understanding of time.

| past | present | future |

THE B-THEORY OF TIME

In distinction from the A-theory, the B-theory does not give a special place to time in general, nor the present in particular. Time is just another dimension in addition to the three conventionally understood dimensions belonging to space. Understood as a unity, spacetime is the four-dimensional space where objects exist. This means that bicycles, flowers, and people exist extended over time in three-dimensional space rather than existing in some version of a privileged present ever moving and shifting to a new time. If the preferred images of the A-theory are a moving spotlight or the direction of an arrow, B-theory can appeal to the individual frames of a video. Just as it is only the combination of all frames which constitutes the reality of a video, so it is all our "parts" temporally extended through the three spatial dimensions as well as time that accounts for us existing as humans.

31

Descartes's *Cogito Ergo Sum*

René Descartes's oft-repeated statement "I think therefore I am" is equally well known in its original Latin, *Cogito ergo sum*. This is perhaps an indication of how familiar and famous the idea is, but just what does it amount to? Certainly, it is not as straightforward as might be supposed from the brevity of the thought.

After all, we utter things like "I am thirsty" or "I am loyal," and we certainly say "I think" quite frequently. So what exactly is Descartes expressing when he says "I think therefore I am"?

DESCARTES AND THE METHOD OF DOUBT

Descartes (1596–1650) formulates his *cogito* in the pages of his *Meditations on First Philosophy*, although he develops the thought in other works as well. The argument for the *cogito* appears in the Second Meditation of the book, where Descartes wants to show that the nature of the human mind is more easily known than that of the body. In the context of this work, an extended discussion of what we can know, Descartes comes up with the *cogito* as a kind of answer to his method of radical doubt. It is a method insofar as Descartes was undertaking to systematically doubt what he previously thought he knew. It was a radical doubt insofar as he was trying to doubt absolutely everything, even so far as to doubt what we normally take for granted as knowledge of the world: that there is a world, that there are objects in the world, and that we are people living in that world. This doubt extended to shape and even body itself, to motion and location. This pursuit of doubt was not merely an academic exercise, as some might suppose, but rather Descartes's very personal acknowledgement of how often he, as a human, fell into error

René Descartes centered the self in thought and not in the body.

and incorrect opinion. Descartes himself stresses the personal nature of his enterprise, as is indicated in the title of his book—"Meditations" rather than the "Disputations" that usually appeared in the titles of philosophical literature of the time. He said that he wanted the reader to come along with him and meditate on the very thoughts he was sharing, so that readers could evaluate these claims for themselves. It should be no surprise in light of this that his *cogito* is centered on the "I" or "ego."

ANSWERING THE DOUBT OF SKEPTICISM

In what sense was the *cogito* a kind of answer to this radical skepticism? First let us look at how Descartes set up the conditions for his radical doubt, so that we can see how his *cogito* is a solution to it. The First Meditation has called into doubt our thoughts that everything around us is real. All things we see in the sky and upon the earth are false, and we falsely believe they exist. Likewise we falsely believe even in our own bodies, that they have flesh and bones.

GOD AND THE EVIL DEMON

We should not expect, he says, given our knowledge of God as good, that God should be responsible for this state of false belief. For such a good God would not allow us to be deceived in this way. Instead, we should imagine that there is some malevolent spirit, commonly called by subsequent philosophers *Descartes's demon* or the *evil demon*, who has concentrated all his power into deceiving us into believing all these falsehoods. If we have all these false beliefs about ourselves and the world because of this evil demon, how do we escape his clutches?

The problem for Descartes was that he needed to find some certain belief to which he could moor his skeptical leanings, an unassailable principle serving as a foundation for all subsequent knowledge. In this sense, the demon was a convenience for arriving at this end. In a famous metaphor, Descartes wished to have in the realm of knowledge what Archimedes with his lever boasted in the realm of mechanics, a point not from which the whole Earth could be moved but from which he could establish all knowledge. The position of radical doubt, remember, has left us without even a trust in the belief that we have bodies, so we are left in a vulnerable position, with very little, it appears, by which we can escape our doubt.

Just as Archimedes had boasted that he only needed a spot from which he could move the world, so Descartes wished to have a solid starting point for thought.

DOUBTING IS A KIND OF THINKING

This is where Descartes's brilliant and yet equally straightforward thoughts on the self and existence start to manifest. For he first brings up the question of whether all this doubt about the world and our bodies causes us—or rather, in the personal phrasing of Descartes, causes *me* in particular—to doubt that we/I exist. The answer is no, since to be convinced of my own existence means that first I must exist. That is, if I am thinking (and this would be true not only in just my own case, but really for anyone or anything that thinks), I would not be able to think if I did not first exist. The act of thinking presupposes that there is someone there, existing, who does the thinking. But Descartes tests this apparent breakthrough into the realm of truth, reminding us of the threat which the evil demon presents, pressing us on whether the demon could not have pressed this belief on us as well. Descartes wants us to consider whether the demon might have made us falsely believe that we exist by the mere fact of thinking. It is here that the brilliance of Descartes shines through. For he says that if we are in fact being deceived, then by virtue of being deceived we are still in fact thinking.

So even in the worst-case scenario of deception by an evil demon, we can have doubts of many and all things, but we cannot doubt that we are thinking. In this way it is necessarily and undoubtedly true that when I think, I am. I cannot doubt my existence, because doubting, as a form of thinking, confirms that I am a doubting, thinking thing, and so I must exist.

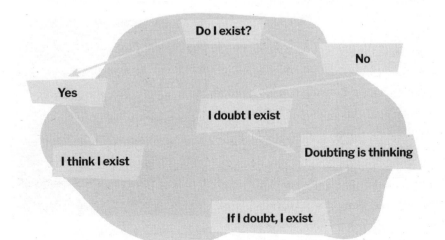

32

Thomas Hobbes's State of Nature

Thomas Hobbes (1588–1679) wished to live a peaceful life, without the threat and actuality of violence. He had lived through the horrors of the English Civil War (1642–51), and in his mind the terrors of a civil war present such a dreadful reality that any form of government is better than living through such a state of violent instability.

But it is hard to secure the kind of situation which prevents civil war. It was this kind of political project for which his book *Leviathan* was designed to give a model.

THE STATE OF NATURE

The natural state of man, as Hobbes construes it, is not a desirable affair. Without laws and power to control the devilish impulses of men, civil society is all but impossible. Murder is actually quite easy to achieve, since even those who are weak can band together in a gang for the purpose of crime, and even a weak person can kill a strong man in a vulnerable moment such as sleep or some other unseen attack. The strong themselves have a natural advantage over the weak, and this might be put to the test by violence. This natural state of vulnerability need not apply only to the prehistorical periods now hidden in the chronicles of time. Rather

Thomas Hobbes had a brutally realistic take on humans in a "natural" state, before political states had been formed.

Commentators have understood the harsh conditions of the English Civil War as giving rise and context to Hobbes's philosophy.

Hobbes insisted it applies to any period that has no established form of government, and which is consequently in dire need of one.

But perhaps you think that Hobbes has overstated his case and that the attractions to murder tempt only the (thankfully few) truly wicked. He has additional arguments which support the idea that the state of nature must be supplanted by the rule of a government. In a state of nature, he argues, we will appeal to violence as a way to get what we want. With no police or army to stop us, we will seek by violence to take what we view is rightfully ours and to violently defend ourselves against what we view as violations of our property and rights. Because this readiness extends to the imagination, fears by themselves are considered sufficient to tilt us toward violence.

THE CONDITIONS FOR SOCIAL STRIFE

On Hobbes's understanding so far, it does not appear that there is room for operating on something like a golden rule, where people treat each other as they want to be treated, and do not treat each other as they do not want to be treated. This is indeed a point that Hobbes cannot concede. But he does think the state of nature gives us a right to self-preservation. Self-preservation bestows upon us the right to guard against death and violence. But this also opens the doors to the judgment of each individual in determining what is and is not threatening enough to require the violence of self-defense. Hobbes denies that there can be any adjudication of these kinds of disputes. He sees the state of nature as a violent, dysfunctional affair, insisting no one can be unjust in this free-for-all. It is unclear why Hobbes says this. Is it because in a state of nature everyone is justified to act in any way from a lack of government, or is it that without a government (and the civil society of which it is a part) humans on their own are unaware and unobservant of the behavior necessary for peace? It is unclear, but for Hobbes, men pop up like mushrooms, he says, from the earth with no connection to each other but mere proximity. In sum, we can say that in Hobbes's judgment there are three causes which intrinsically give rise to this uncivilized strife. Competition of people with each other, seeking glory or reputation of one kind or another, and an overall lack of faith in each other.

THE LEVIATHAN RISES

As mentioned at the beginning, it is this state of nature, with its necessary gruesomeness, that Hobbes wants to avoid. This is not merely a prudential avoidance but a moral demand: the state of nature is so wicked that we are obligated in practice to avoid it. As a part of this rather gloomy conception of the human condition, Hobbes also believes in other laws of nature. These laws, of which Hobbes lists 19, are rationally discovered and preserve life on the one hand and prohibit that which destroys life on the other. The first of these laws reiterates the need to find peace as the first resort, and only after this has failed to resort to war. This desire for peace so overtakes us that natural man actually lays aside rights to all things with the goal of social freedom. The intent of this dramatic move is to bestow upon some one entity, whether one person or some collective, all the power which collectively the people held for themselves in a state of nature. The people, in acknowledgement of their desperate need for order and peace, subordinate their natural freedom to this

Why is the state of nature so "nasty, brutish, and short" among men?

➤➤ **Competition for goods**

➤➤ **Pursuit of glory**

➤➤ **Suspicion and mistrust**

The Leviathan rises when individuals have consented to concede power to a unitary state.

political order. This political entity is called by Hobbes a commonwealth, or a *Leviathan*. The individuals of this state pledge their obedience to the commonwealth in a type of exchange—the state gaining power and the people ensured of safety. The only right preserved in this drastic transfer of power is the right to self-defense in case of bodily harm.

It is this transfer of power to some political magistrate, a Leviathan, which is depicted as a collection of people in a single giant King, portrayed on the cover of Hobbes's book *Leviathan*. This same image serves as a good illustration of the social contract which it represents. If some political power is necessary to control men in their natural state, and this political power is established and maintained only by the consent of people, then it seems reasonable to think that men must abide by this agreement to maintain the power of the commonwealth so that the violent state of nature is avoided. If the Leviathan falls, so do they.

33

George Berkeley's
Esse Est Percipi

George Berkeley (1685–1753) presents an interesting figure
in the history of philosophy. He was not only Bishop of Cloyne
in the Anglican Church of Ireland, but his religious convictions
contributed much to the formulation of his famous maxim
esse est percipi (to exist is to be perceived). Berkeley's focus
of attack was on the rather conventional claim that material
objects exist.

He thought that belief in material objects, objects which do not depend
on minds, leads to skepticism and, more dangerously and ultimately,
atheism. If material objects do exist independent of minds, then there
is no role for God, since he is the divine mind, so Berkeley sought to
demonstrate that the only things which do exist are the ideas we have
in our minds.

ALL WE PERCEIVE ARE OUR IDEAS OF THINGS
Berkeley's tactic for attacking belief in material objects first begins to
show itself when he distinguishes two separate elements in the way
we perceive. He says that when we perceive objects, such as tables or
trees, what we have is our idea or perception of them, and that is all we
have. We do not possess the table itself in our mind but only the idea
of the table. We might think we are perceiving an object, but what we
are really perceiving is an idea. As we will see, Berkeley will not even
grant that we are perceiving an object in the world. He will limit himself
to admit we perceive an idea merely, for all we perceive are ideas. The
trick in understanding Berkeley's argumentative strategy, to convince
us that all things we perceive are ideas, is his identification of what we
see with our very ideas. The tree is nothing more than what we perceive,

Geo. Berkeley S.T.P.
Dec. Derensis.

Like many philosophers before the modern era, Berkeley was also a theologian, and his philosophy was partly an attempt to justify belief in God.

be that seeing its pyramidal shape, hearing its leaves, or smelling the bark and roots.

To approach this in another way, Berkeley is not saying that the way we perceive a tree, for example, is that we have a perception of it, and that this perception refers to the real tree. This would understand perception as being a type of medium or relationship between the tree and our understanding. On that understanding, which Berkeley denies, let us call the tree C, and our perception of it B, while we ourselves are A. So B (perception) stands between C (the tree) and A (ourselves). What Berkeley claims instead is that B and C are simply the same things. A perception does not refer to the tree because the perception is nothing other than the tree itself.

PERCEPTIONS ARE NOT REPRESENTATIONAL

The account which Berkeley is opposing is a representational understanding of perception. This representational understanding means that there are objects out there in the world and the role of our perception is to represent them, in some fashion or another, in our mind. For Berkeley it is simply impossible for this type of representation to occur. For representation is a kind of likeness, similarity, or resemblance, and an idea can only be like another idea, it cannot be like something material.

We don't see an object itself, but an *image* of that object.

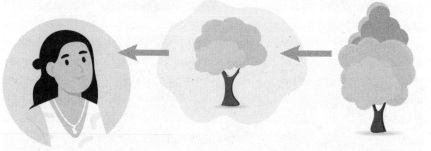

IDEAS ARE ONLY LIKE OTHER IDEAS

Why is it that an idea can only be like another idea, and an idea cannot be like some physical object? We can say two things. One is to make a claim about how we could come to know, or even verify, the fact that some external physical object resembles our perception or idea of it. We could never directly compare what a tree, as a material object, is like in relation to our idea of it, for our idea of it exhausts our relationship or understanding of the tree. Berkeley also seems to think that a representational form of understanding is just contradictory and absurd. A physical object is a physical object, and a perception is a perception. So how could a physical object be compared to a thought? There is nothing in common between these fundamentally different kinds of things.

COMMON SENSE AND BERKELEY

So far, Berkeley seems to have offered us a radical proposal, opposed to our normal understanding and our common experience. We experience objects and their properties all the time. Don't we feel the hardness of a stone, hear the chimes of a church bell, taste the sweetness of grapes, see the size of this house, and so on? Don't all these qualities belong to these physical objects? Berkeley counters this by reminding you that all of these so-called qualities arise as perceptions in the mind, and so properly belong to the mind.

There may be a reason that our common sense is drawn to a representational picture of how our minds work. For example, when we go through a doorway, it seems that our minds are representing to us that a doorway is over here, with a door and a handle, and if we turn and pull the handle appropriately, we can pass through the door. And we perform actions like this often. Berkeley says that if there really is a doorway and door out there in the world, how is it that something physical, a door, could cause the thought of a door, in my immaterial mind, to arise? This is a claim that the very nature of the physical and mental, being opposed as the material to the immaterial, can never interact because of their fundamental and unbridgeable differences. This point about the interaction of physical objects and immaterial ideas is akin to the argument referenced above about similarity. Just as there would have to be some independent point of comparison between matter and idea, so also there must be some independent point of contact for physical objects and their ideas to interact, so that objects could cause ideas in the mind to form.

The comprehensive nature of ideas and how they permeate our thinking is shown by what is often called the *master argument*. You say, offers Berkeley, that you can imagine a tree existing apart from a mind, but in the process of imagination you yourself are forming an idea, showing that everything, even when we try to conceive of it apart from the mind, is dependent on our minds.

The "Master Argument"

➡ Berkeley says that the only things that exist are the perceptions of objects, not the objects themselves.

➡ If you agree, then the mind is all that exists.

➡ If you disagree, you are using your mind to imagine that objects exist apart from the mind. But this thought happens in the mind, so objects are in the mind as well.

34

David Hume's Causal Inference

David Hume (1711–76) was historically a very influential philosopher, although his views are mostly unknown to the public. We will discuss his famous critique of how people arrive at what they think is a relation between cause and effect. Cause and effect, as well as our perception of when something is a cause or an effect, has wide application to our everyday lives. If Hume's theories were to undermine this concept, it would have dire consequences for what we think we know and even how we live.

EMPIRICISM AND "IDEAS"

First, Hume was an empiricist. This means that he believed all knowledge ultimately derived from sense perceptions. He divided our mental content into two rough categories, the first of which is *impressions*, which includes perceptions but also love, hate, desire, and will. The second category is *thoughts* or *ideas*. Ideas are dependent upon and so derived from our impressions. Basically, ideas extract something from impressions, and formulate something new from them. As the illustration on page 148 shows, impressions are distinct and different from ideas, although it needs to be kept in mind that while ideas originate from impressions, they "break free," so to speak, and stand on their own. Seeing a shiny yellow nugget newly taken from a mine is an example of an impression. An idea (again, remember, it's dependent on the impression) is the concept of "gold" which we apply to this shiny yellow nugget. It is important to recognize that the application of this concept (or label) "gold" is not something inherent in the mere perception itself. It is something we add to our perception of the shiny yellow nugget. This can best be understood if we think of how we apply this idea of gold as a general concept to other things, and how we can even confer it on imaginary objects, such as conceiving of a golden mountain.

THE UNIFORMITY PRINCIPLE OF CAUSE AND EFFECT

There is one way in which we can transcend the limitation of our impressions or senses. This is where

"Gold" is not something in the perception itself, but a description we add to the nugget.

the formation of cause and effect comes into play. Cause and effect is based on our experience of previous examples. We saw the sun rise three days ago, two days ago, and today, and so we form a conception that each day the sun rises. There is an additional factor in this experience, which Hume called *conjunction*. The beginning of the day is frequently conjoined with the rising of the sun, and on this basis we think that when tomorrow begins, the sun also will rise. This tendency toward regularity is called the *Uniformity Principle*. It is this Uniformity Principle at which Hume aims his critical judgment.

So how does Hume attack the Uniformity Principle, when a constant conjunction between two different events, like the beginning of the day and the sunrise, means that we think there is a cause-and-effect relationship? He divides reasoning into two kinds, *Relations of Ideas* and *Matters of Fact*. *Relations of Ideas* includes mathematical concepts, and any others like them which result in a demonstrative certainty. It is in this sense that $1 + 1 = 2$ is demonstratively certain, and since "1" is a concept derived from experience or an impression, such as from counting our fingers or pebbles, we consider "1" an idea in Hume's technical usage. 1, an idea, is combined with 1, an idea, in a particular relationship and so in this sense we can consider this simple mathematical proposition a relation of ideas. The other type of reasoning is *Matters of Fact*. These are distinguished from Relations of Ideas in that they are observed directly from nature. Most relevant in this distinction is that they can be imagined to be otherwise than they are without any fear of contradiction. A mathematical truth of a Relation of Ideas cannot possibly be otherwise than it is, for $1 + 1 = 2$ is necessarily true. On the other hand, we can easily imagine that the sun will not rise tomorrow, because there is no contradiction if we conceive a sunrise not occurring tomorrow. Another way in which Hume describes these two types of reasoning is that Relations of Ideas are necessary while Matters are Fact are probable.

WHERE DO CAUSE AND EFFECT COME FROM?

Hume says that our notion of cause and effect must fit into either Relations of Ideas or Matters of Fact. There is not another category into which cause and effect can fit. Going back a little earlier, we can also say that cause and effect is not an impression, because it is not something we grasp with our eyes alone but is something added to an impression.

So, if cause and effect, understood as the Uniformity Principle, fits into either Relations of Ideas or Matters of Fact, Hume asks, where does it fit? First, he says it cannot belong to a relation of ideas because to this category belong only things which necessarily are as they are. It is impossible for $1 + 1 = 2$ to not be true, but this is not true for the Uniformity Principle. Another way of stating this is to repeat what was said above in the case of the sun not rising, and to broaden and generalize the thought. This is to say that there is no contradiction in thinking that whereas normally the phenomenon of B follows A, we can easily imagine that this does not happen. If the Uniformity Principle does not belong to the Relations of Ideas, then this leaves only Matters of Fact. As we have seen, Matters of Fact concern things or events which can be otherwise than they are without fear of contradiction. Hume points out that the

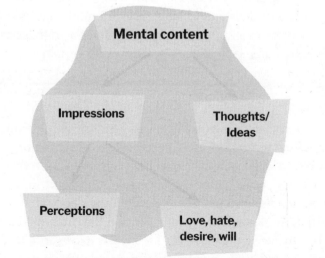

reasoning behind the category of Matters of Fact is probable—that is, based upon the principle that the future will resemble the past. What this shows, according to Hume, is that our notion of cause and effect takes for granted or merely assumes the Uniformity Principle, since the Uniformity Principle simply is our articulation of cause and effect. Thus we are not justified in our reasoning about cause and effect because it is simply assumed and is not founded on independent argument. The conclusion is that we are not justified in our belief in the Uniformity Principle, or cause and effect, but instead we just assume it to be true, when at best it is just probable or likely.

Two Kinds of Reasoning

Relations of ideas (shown with certainty and are necessary) e.g. mathematical concepts like addition

Matters of fact (not shown with certainty and are probable) e.g. trees grow vertically upwards, stones are solid

35

Marx's Historical Materialism

Karl Marx (1818–83) evokes many reactions. His writings on politics and philosophy, often touching on religious and cultural issues, have gained him as many admirers as critics. He was educated as a philosopher, and we can see his work on philosophy reflected in his thoughts on history and political science, ultimately leading to his theory of communism. The heart of his theorizing is centered in what we call historical materialism.

THE MATERIAL CAUSES OF HISTORICAL MATERIALISM

Historical materialism starts from the premise that matter is all there is. As an atheist Marx was committed to materialism, and this belief may have been formed in part by research on his doctoral thesis, which was a comparative analysis of natural, as opposed to supernatural, explanations in Ancient Greek philosophy. This focus on the material conditions of life is important to correctly understanding Marx, for unlike almost every philosophical predecessor, he claimed that material conditions of society give rise to the way people think and act, as opposed to forms of human thinking giving rise to society. This distinguishes him from Hegel, by whom he was influenced heavily in singling out dialectic (see page 185) as an important force in history. Of course, Marx shifted focus away from ideas to matter as the driving force behind economic and political change.

These material forces which garner so much philosophical attention from Marx are more specifically identified as the means or forces of production. The *means of production*, or factors which play into the production of material goods, is a term used to capture the broad array of tools, machines, facilities, factories, and raw materials which, when combined with human knowledge, produce economic goods and services. In brief, the means of production are the means to bring about economic goods and services, understood as material sources utilized by human knowledge by means of technology.

THE TIERS OF MARX'S THEORY

Marx's theory is a bottom-up kind of theory. The absolute foundation is materialism because the material conditions—that is, the availability of raw material and the other factors in the means of production— accounts for the structure of a society's economy. The structure of the economy in turn gives form to the structure of the social institutions of society. This second level of social structure is often referred to as the superstructure. The social institutions which comprise the superstructure are religious, political, philosophical, and legal in nature. It is at this level that the stratification of different classes in society comes to be. On the one hand, the nature of the relationship between the economic structure and the social superstructure is between cause and effect, since the economic is prior to and explains the structure of the social. On the other hand, the economic structure and the social superstructure are mutually reinforcing. This is because while the economic gives rise to the social, people operating at the level of the social superstructure seek at the same time to stabilize the economic level, since disrupting the economic conditions will cause the social structure to change or even be abolished. It seems that Marx still wanted to allow for the possibility that some

Karl Marx built his philosophy from the ground up, focusing on the material conditions which give rise to society.

elements of the superstructure were not conditioned by the economic terms on the ground. So literature, for example, is not an expression of the economic structure of a society, but independently expresses its own goals.

Alongside these structures of a society, Marx thought that the productive power of society has a tendency to increase over time. When production begins to stagnate and is no longer progressing and increasing, Marx believed that this structure will inevitably be subject to revolution in which it is not only overthrown but replaced by a structure which can provide for an increase in production.

Means of production   **Human knowledge**

+

=

**Economic goods
and services**

Structure of the economy

creates & forms

supports & reinforces

Superstructure (religious, political, philosophical, legal structure)

THE STAGES OF HISTORY

Marx's historical materialism was not wholly a theoretical expression, taken out of thin air. It was formed from an analysis of history divided into stages. The first is the tribal. In the tribal stage, the most basic, the organization of society is merely an enlargement of the domestic state, with men hunting and women tending to the home. At the second stage of slave society, the earliest forms of a class society arise. Ancient Egypt, Greece, and Rome are examples of this type of society. The third stage is feudal society. In this society the various classes have rights, but slaves are treated as property. The main means of production is agricultural, with serfs providing most of the labor. After the feudal stage comes capitalism, where capitalists produce goods that can be used for exchange. Historical examples of this shift from the feudal to the capitalist include the English Revolution of 1640–60 and the French Revolution in 1789.

CLASS DIVISION

Marx is famous for his statement that "the history of all hitherto existing societies is the history of class struggles." This concept of class conflict can also be observed alongside the historical stages described above. The basic idea is that in slave societies, slaves are the oppressed class and the master is the oppressor, and in feudal societies serfs and lords fulfill essentially the same roles. In capitalist societies this dichotomy between a dominating minority and an exploited class has been somewhat obscured—but is revealed as the relationship between employer and employees. Capitalism fails in this regard to establish liberty and equality as evidenced by the wealth hoarded by an elite upper class. Eventually this stage will give way to a communist stage, when the lower class seizes power. The eventuality of communism will give rise to a society in which every person receives as he is in need and contributes as he is able, leading a life independent of the struggles of a working class as we know it today, but pursuing those meaningful activities which the choice of leisure may allow.

The French Revolution is a textbook example of the shift from a feudal to a capitalist society.

36

John Rawls's Veil of Ignorance

From childhood on through to our adult years, we all have a concept of fairness as a desirable aspect of human life. The *veil of ignorance* is a concept attempting to give a place to fairness in our political practice. It was proposed by John Rawls (1921–2002) in his book *A Theory of Justice*. Before I explain what the veil amounts to and why Rawls thought it was necessary, let's look first at how it fits into his broader notion of justice in a political setting.

THE ORIGINAL POSITION

Rawls wanted to consider a way in which justice in the political sphere could be achieved without prejudice. The impartiality he had in mind would be an antidote to the social bigotries found in societies that excluded unpopular groups or individuals from certain rights or privileges, harming these people in the process. He named the process of deliberation which results in this form of justice the *original position*.

In the original position, what we are to imagine is that a group of average people are hidden behind a veil of ignorance. This is not a real physical veil. The purpose of this veil is to shield each person from knowledge of his or her particularities such as race, social class, sex and other similar factors. Stripped of the knowledge of these attributes, Rawls thought, people would not be prone to bestow rights or privileges upon one group simply because they happened to belong to that group. If I imagine I don't know, for example, whether I am a man or a woman, then I will not be tempted to confer special rights on men at the expense of women, because under the veil of ignorance I might be a woman. Let us be clear: the veil of ignorance and the original position are hypothetical

Original Position

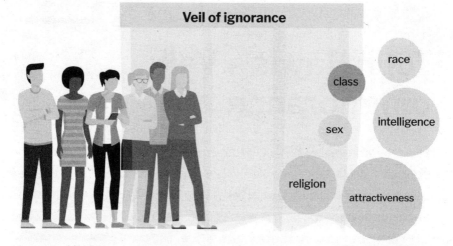

situations envisioned as a means to clarify our thoughts about the political process. However, Rawls thought that such a hypothetical conception was in line with philosophical precedents offered by philosophers such as Hobbes and Locke.

THE CONDITIONS OF THE ORIGINAL POSITION

In typical circumstances people in society choose principles for political systems on the basis of a self-interest often based on their own membership in groups such as sex or race. The veil would prompt different choices. What principles would people without knowledge of their own circumstances choose? Rawls thought that this would induce people to choose those principles which would be the most fair and the most impartial for all. After all, without knowing to which group one belongs, there is no incentive to form a society favoring a group to which one might *not* belong, and more to the point, to disfavor or even significantly harm another group to which one *does* happen to belong. It is doubtful, if not impossible, that people with this veil of ignorance would agree that only one race could vote or own property, if in fact they did not know to which race they belonged. People are disinterested in a good way because they are unaware of what their interests are. Thus there is a conception of the original position as transcending the interests of individuality so that it can shift the political enterprise as a united social project. The original position, whatever else it is, is a kind of social contract.

John Rawls's political philosophy has been highly influential in the last 40 years.

THE PRINCIPLE OF EQUAL LIBERTY

If people were presented with all the alternatives to be taken from history and political science, Rawls thought that there were two principles which people would decide upon in this original position: the *Equal Liberty Principle* and the *Principle of Equal Opportunity*. The Equal Liberty Principle affirms that every person has a right to a set of basic liberties and rights. The Principle of Equal Opportunity is more complex, but its aim is to limit the ways in which social and economic inequalities can arise in a just state. We will return to this principle, but first we should look at the Principle of Equal Opportunity in more detail.

THE PRINCIPLE OF EQUAL OPPORTUNITY

What kind of liberties does the Principle of Equal Opportunity protect? Freedom of speech or thought; personal liberty as an individual, such as freedom from slavery and the ability to choose one's occupation; and legal liberties and rights. The possession and distribution of these rights is based purely on being a person in society, and no other grounds.

The Principle of Equal Opportunity is related to and is dependent upon the first, Equal Liberty. In general terms what Equal Opportunity is trying to recognize is that disparities of one kind or another occur, so we should try to ensure that the disparities which do arise are fair. How does Rawls think his principle can promote fairness? The principle has several parts. What these different aspects share is that they concern in one way or another a distribution of external goods. External goods of this type most commonly are going to be certain occupations or incomes, but they can apply to power or influence. So one thing Rawls wants to guard against in these circumstances is that these goods are not reserved for certain people based on irrelevant criteria such as their gender or race. Another aspect to this principle, also concerned with protecting the less privileged, is that disparities are tolerated provided that they allow for improving the life of the least advantaged persons in a society. To take the example of someone earning a huge salary—say as the manager of a professional sports team—this would be permitted under the principle only if this salary could somehow benefit the least privileged people in that culture, either monetarily or by some other means. One result ensured by this is that the disparity between the privileged and underprivileged—or in this case, between the rich and poor—is not increased more than is necessary.

The Equal Liberty Principle and Principle of Equal Opportunity both operate under an individual's conception of the human good. If someone wants to pursue a certain career, she may do so, provided she does not violate either of the principles. So there is room for earning a high salary or having a lot of political power, provided that everyone equally has a shot at these positions and the least well-off are benefited by this state of affairs.

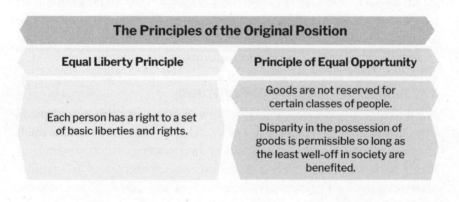

The Principles of the Original Position	
Equal Liberty Principle	**Principle of Equal Opportunity**
	Goods are not reserved for certain classes of people.
Each person has a right to a set of basic liberties and rights.	Disparity in the possession of goods is permissible so long as the least well-off in society are benefited.

37

Gettier Problems

There is a state of the human mind, we think and assure ourselves, that we call knowledge. But how do we know that we know? What are the conditions that need to be fulfilled to say that we, or someone else, possess knowledge? Edmund Gettier (1927–2021) was engaging with these types of issues when he wrote his paper "Is Justified True Belief Knowledge?"

Before looking at his captivating examples, we should first look at the theory of justified true belief which he was calling into question.

WHAT IS JUSTIFIED TRUE BELIEF?

Justified true belief is a theory about knowledge which has some intuitive appeal. At its most fundamental, it is a theory proposing necessary and sufficient conditions for when knowledge has been achieved. When these conditions are met, we can say that someone has knowledge. We commonly make a distinction between belief and knowledge. We say that we *know* our house is white, but we *believe* that the marriage of the newly-wed couple will last. The distinguishing feature between belief and knowledge is not the degree of importance. We probably care more for the survival of a marriage than the paint of a house. Nor does the difference necessarily depend on the conviction with which we hold it, as we could say that we believe in God with much more enthusiasm and commitment than saying we know our houses are white. Rather the difference between knowledge and belief, at least in this portrayal, is one of degrees. Knowledge has a higher degree of certainty than belief.

If this relationship of knowledge to belief is true, there is a sense in which knowledge is a kind of belief, in that one must believe what one knows. When we get to the Gettier problems themselves, we will explore this relationship more closely. Now we turn to the *truth* condition of justified true belief. Truth refers not to what we think, whether that be knowledge or belief, but to the state of actual affairs, whether in reality something actually is. So the truth of whether my house is white depends not on whether I believe it is white, nor even on whether I know it to be white, but only on whether it is actually white.

The last condition of *justification* is introduced to guarantee that the first two elements of knowledge, the true belief, are assented to for the right reasons. Holding true belief for the correct reason means that I come to hold the belief in the proper way, which does not come about merely by chance or by luck. So if a friend tells me that she has just got a pet dog without telling me the breed, and that night I have a dream that she bought a cocker spaniel, I cannot claim that my belief in her possession of a spaniel is justified. This is the case even if she does turn out to have a spaniel. There is an acknowledgement that a justified reason for believing my friend bought a spaniel would be, among other possibilities, that either she told me of the spaniel or I saw the dog with my own eyes. To have a dream in which, by pure happenstance, she appeared to have a cocker spaniel is not justification for my belief that she has such a dog.

GETTIER CRITIQUES JUSTIFIED TRUE BELIEF

An account of knowledge, following the above conditions, must be justified true belief in the ways specified. It is a theory very much like this that Gettier was critiquing when he introduced his problems. The introduction of these problems was designed to show that even if these conditions are fulfilled, knowledge has not been achieved. Justification and truth, combined with belief, are not sufficient to establish knowledge.

THE CASE OF SMITH AND JONES

The first situation Gettier described is a little unusual. Imagine a man named Smith who is in line for a promotion, though there is one other candidate, Jones. Smith is really eager to win this new job but there is a considerable piece of evidence that factors in his disfavor. The company

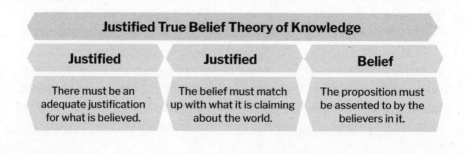

Justified True Belief Theory of Knowledge		
Justified	**Justified**	**Belief**
There must be an adequate justification for what is believed.	The belief must match up with what it is claiming about the world.	The proposition must be assented to by the believers in it.

president has told Smith that Jones will in fact be the eventual winner of the promotion. It also happens that on this very same morning Smith has paid Jones in the form of 10 coins that he owed him. So Smith knows, because he saw him place the money in his pocket, that Jones has these 10 coins in his pants. Combining what the president told him, that Jones will get the job, with his knowledge of 10 coins in Jones's pocket, Smith thinks to himself, "The man with 10 coins in his pocket will get the job." So far, there is no logical problem in this rather strange scenario. Smith is justified in thinking that the man with 10 coins in his pocket will get the job.

Now this is where Gettier makes the account interesting for claims about knowledge and justified true belief. It turns out, despite what the president told Smith, that Jones will not in fact get the job. Smith will be the lucky recipient of the promotion. One more piece of relevant information is that it has escaped Smith's notice that he also has 10 coins in his own pocket. If we examine Smith's line of reasoning, we see that he had justified true belief. He had a belief, "The man with 10 coins in his pocket will get the job," and it was justified, since the president of the company, a credible source, gave him the information which led to this belief, and it was true, because the man with 10 coins in his pocket did get the job. Yet despite these all being true, we would not say Smith possessed knowledge.

A SIMPLE EXAMPLE OF A GETTIER PROBLEM

For a simpler example, imagine someone looking out of a car window and seeing a fluffy white animal grazing on the grass. On this description

Is the person justified in thinking there is a sheep standing on the hill?

she is justified in thinking she sees a sheep. Unbeknown to her, it is not actually a sheep, but only a cardboard cut-out of a sheep. Yet an actual sheep is, in fact, hiding behind this cardboard. It turns out, but merely by luck, that this woman had a justified true belief in thinking she saw a sheep. Yet it is hard to say she *knew* she saw a sheep.

These and other so-called Gettier problems have flourished, showing that justified true belief is not knowledge, that there is something beyond these conditions which accounts for knowledge.

38

Thomas Kuhn's Concept of Revolutions

Philosophy of Science as a free-standing subject within the discipline of philosophy is a relatively modern field, taking root only quite recently in the twentieth century. It would be mistaken, however, to think that this means the subject matter is somehow unimportant or peripheral.

In fact, it can be precisely because something is so important and fundamental to how we see the world that we take it for granted. It is so conceptually basic that it is hidden from us, being a part of the various assumptions by which we judge and perceive everything else.

KNOWLEDGE AND THEORY

Thomas Kuhn (1922–96) had something very much like this in his mind when he formulated his ideas on the progress of science in *The Structure of Scientific Revolutions*. He begins by arguing is that there is never such as thing as science, bare and naked by itself, which takes uninterpreted facts and explains them. In fact, normal science has assumptions, a set of beliefs and practices which it has taken on from the past, and all information has been filtered through these assumptions. This is not to assign an inexcusable prejudice to the practices of science, but is instead an acknowledgement that information, which science builds upon, does not speak for itself. To put this into scientific idiom, there must be a theory into which we can fit and so explain our results and observations.

Thomas Kuhn's concept of a "paradigm shift" has entered into common usage.

163

The paradigm of natural selection is a context for explaining finch beak variation.

THEORIES AND PARADIGMS

Theory in this sense can be as simple as using a single scientific achievement to guide research. An example of such an achievement is the theory of natural selection as introduced by Charles Darwin, which served as a basis for subsequent scientists in further scientific investigation. Because the idea of natural selection can serve this role, Kuhn dubbed this a *paradigm*. A paradigm is the scientific model under which a given science or part of that science is practiced, in this example the theory of natural selection. A scientific paradigm is necessary to make sense of the subject under examination. So the variation of finch beaks on the Galapagos Islands is explained in the paradigm of natural selection by pointing out how each beak is adapted by natural selection toward a specific way of eating, cracking nuts or extracting insects as appropriate for the species.

As paradigms continue with explanatory success, they become more widespread. This means they become more well defined and gather a precision they did not have at the beginning. Problems with fitting the data or raw information into the paradigm also arise. These are comparable to puzzles within the framework of the scientific paradigm, items which need to be solved and understood within this larger framework.

ANOMALIES AND PARADIGMS

In addition to the world of puzzles—that is, difficulties which present themselves to a given paradigm but are solved—and normal research which furthers the paradigm, there are anomalies. These anomalies come about through the normal process of discovery which happens during scientific investigation. The problem which surfaces in an anomaly is that it simply cannot be explained in the current paradigm. Just as significantly, all paradigms have their own anomalies. Sometimes a persistent anomaly is resolved into the paradigm, but sometimes if the anomaly becomes significant enough, it presents a kind of crisis for the paradigm.

THE CRISIS OF A PARADIGM

So, a crisis of a paradigm can be brought about by some inexplicable anomaly, which is unable to be solved or explained by this theoretical framework, and the circumstances of this crisis are often measured in longer periods of time. Since the present paradigm cannot solve the anomaly, a new paradigm with new rules is constructed in order to explain it. If this new paradigm is successful in explaining the anomaly in a way that the old one was not, it is possible that the new paradigm will supplant the old one.

PARADIGM SHIFTS

If in fact there is a transition to a new paradigm, then this replacement occurs either in whole or in part, because the new paradigm is incompatible with the old paradigm. Kuhn compares this replacement to what happens in a political revolution when the members of a political community grow dissatisfied with the current regime—a parallel that reiterates how paradigms are incompatible. Either one or the other must be chosen. If there is an adoption of a new paradigm and a rejection of the old, Kuhn

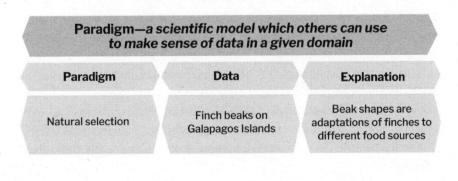

Paradigm—a scientific model which others can use to make sense of data in a given domain		
Paradigm	**Data**	**Explanation**
Natural selection	Finch beaks on Galapagos Islands	Beak shapes are adaptations of finches to different food sources

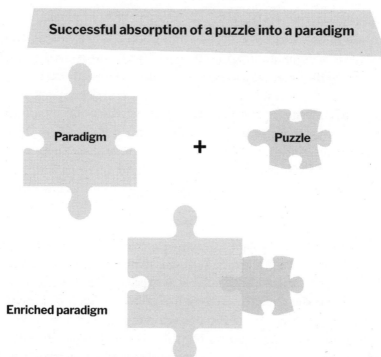

calls this a revolution. He also calls this, in a phrase which has gained wide currency, a *paradigm shift*.

As the name "revolution" implies, a scientific revolution can create a radical change in how people view the world. It is a scientific revolution but also a perceptual and mental revolution. So whereas biologists before Darwin were perhaps inclined to ignore the hips of whales, after him they were interested in interpreting these skeletal structures in the light of evolution, and came to interpret them as vestigial and primordial remnants of a far-off ancestor. This makes total sense in light of how we saw earlier that paradigms are necessary in order to process and understand data. If information does not speak for itself, but must be interpreted and filtered through some lens, then it is all the more true that changing lenses means we will see previous things in a new way and also things that are entirely new.

PROGRESS IN SCIENCE

The last issue which Kuhn deals with is the concept of progress, in light of what he has said about revolutions. He thinks that progress is very closely associated with the idea of science, to the degree that it may even be part of its definition. Nevertheless, it may be surprising to learn that Kuhn does not think that paradigm shifts lead scientists closer to the truth. Rather, what he says is that our practices of science become more refined, detailed, and explanatory.

Paradigm Shift

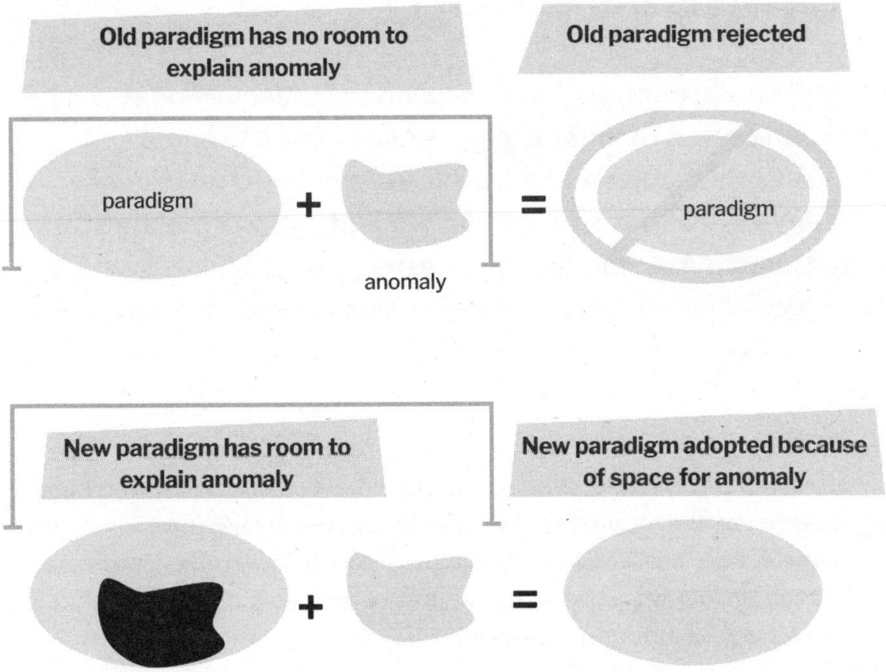

Old paradigm has no room to explain anomaly

paradigm + anomaly = paradigm

Old paradigm rejected

New paradigm has room to explain anomaly

+ =

New paradigm adopted because of space for anomaly

39

John Searle's Chinese Room

John Searle (born 1932) introduced the Chinese Room experiment, a thought experiment designed to argue against the notion that a machine can possess intelligence in any meaningful way. The experiment is closely related to the question of whether or not a machine can think, and in particular whether a computer could ever pass the Turing Test.

The Turing Test essentially boils down to testing whether the intelligence of a computer can be distinguished from that of a human. Since a human is the judge, the requirement for discerning this intelligence is not that a computer can actually have a human mind, whatever that would mean, but rather that it is, at minimum, able to imitate a human mind to the satisfaction of a human observer.

A SKETCH OF THE CHINESE ROOM

Searle's Chinese Room gives a more sophisticated account than is strictly necessary, but it can be simplified to bring out the heart of the experiment. The setup for the Chinese Room is fairly straightforward, even if a bit unusual. Imagine that you speak only one language: English. You are sitting by yourself in a room with a significant amount of Chinese texts. These Chinese texts are divided up so that they can be used by you in writing Chinese. In addition, you have a sort of rulebook, in English, for matching up various kinds of Chinese. Now, since you do not actually know a single bit of Chinese, Chinese characters will appear to you to be nothing more than symbols or strange drawings. The English rulebook will give you directions on how to answer in Chinese when given questions in Chinese, although as you experience it, this will involve matching one symbol to another in the rulebook, without any conscious

John Searle conceived of a thought experiment to show that computers cannot think or have intelligence.

comprehension of what is going on in Chinese. Thus the rulebook is not translating for your benefit, not telling you that this character means "flower" and that one means "car," much less the meaning of phrases or sentences. The whole process is opaque to you. You are doing no more than copying pictures as the rulebook guides you.

After all this, the dramatic moment occurs. As you are in the room alone, a messenger opens the door and gives you something that has just been written in Chinese from someone outside the room. Now you set to work. You take one set of symbols (as the Chinese appears to you) and using the rulebook, you correlate these symbols to another set of symbols, other Chinese characters which will serve as your answer to what has been given to you. The messenger returns and retrieves your answer and gives it to the person outside the room who made the original message. This process continues and you end up having a long-running dialogue with the person on the outside.

THE CHINESE ROOM DOES NOT REQUIRE UNDERSTANDING

It is clear, as described, that you have absolutely no comprehension of what the meaning or content of the Chinese is, not even whether it is an involved story, a job interview or just frivolous small talk. What you are doing involves no understanding at all of Chinese, and Searle says this is no different in fact from the process of a computer or machine. A machine is able only to *do as it is told*—that is, depend upon rules which it follows, in the form of code or a program, and this too requires no understanding on the computer's part of what it is doing. Just as we do not understand Chinese, but still can successfully give the correct answers in Chinese in this thought experiment, a computer can successively give the right answers and output when it is given certain inputs or questions, provided that it has, so to speak, a digital rulebook it can follow.

From Searle's perspective the Chinese Room shows that it is not only in simple cases that a computer does not *know* what it is doing, since it is only mechanically following rules, but that in principle this point will apply to even the most robust claims of computer artificial intelligence. There is something over and above merely correctly manipulating data that needs to be accounted for when we think of intelligence. A computer does not know, think, or understand, it obeys in rote fashion, and it is impossible that it could ever come to possess these abilities as long as it is merely following rules. What's more, it is too much to ask that computers not operate in the fashion they do, as it is fundamental to the definition of a machine or computer that the rules of a program must be followed.

ANSWERS TO SEARLE'S CHINESE ROOM

One answer to the Chinese Room experiment is acknowledging the ignorance of the person who does the manipulation while claiming that understanding is achieved at a higher level. Although it would be true that the person doing the manipulation of symbols is ignorant, the *whole* of the Chinese Room—considered with all the texts, rulebook, the person, and so forth—does understand what is going on. Searle does not think this a good objection, as he says the man could memorize all the information from the rulebook so that he is not dependent upon anything external. Even though he kept all this information in his head, the man would still not know Chinese, since he did not know what any of these symbols meant.

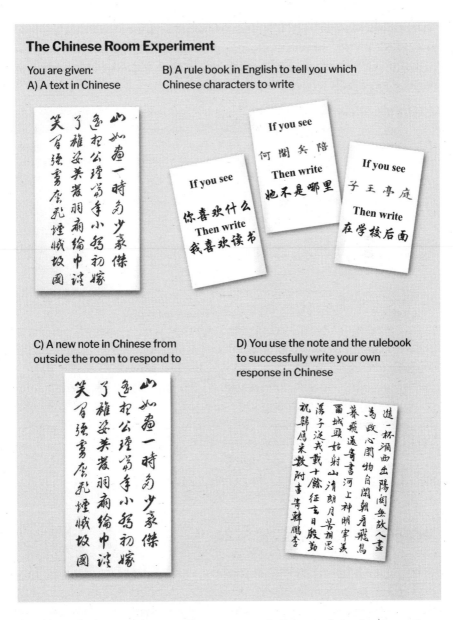

The Chinese Room Experiment

You are given:
A) A text in Chinese

B) A rule book in English to tell you which Chinese characters to write

C) A new note in Chinese from outside the room to respond to

D) You use the note and the rulebook to successfully write your own response in Chinese

The Chinese Room invokes issues relating to thought, intention, consciousness, and awareness. Is being aware of what we are doing central to understanding what we are doing? It seems we take this for granted. It brings out the fact that when we are talking about what goes on *inside* a computer, just as when we talk about the mind of a person, these mental activities are hidden from us. So, in the case of computers, we are prone to make analogous comparisons from our experience.

This also shows that even in a situation where we are observing another person, we do not have access to his or her thoughts, and so what seem to be actions done with understanding might turn out to be only someone performing a task without comprehension.

40

David Chalmers's Philosophical Zombies

What is a zombie, we may ask. Beyond the grotesque horror which these creatures evoke in books and films, philosophers have also appealed to them as a way to show that there is something beyond the mere physical. Popular depictions certainly play up the physical aspect, as zombies are no more than mindless revivified flesh and bone.

The philosophical use of zombies is similar, highlighting this feature of mindlessness to imagine how and if we as humans are made up of anything beside flesh, bones, blood, and pulsing neurons.

ZOMBIES AS AN OBJECTION TO MATERIALISM

Philosophical zombies are used as a counterexample, an example whose existence by itself forms an objection against another belief or argument. A counterexample to the claim that "all birds fly" is penguins. All by itself the example of a penguin is thought sufficient to refute the first claim. In the case of zombies, they are used as a counterexample to the idea of materialism or physicalism. Materialism, simply stated, is the belief that everything that exists is made of matter, or is physical. Materialism excludes the possibility of invisible and immaterial souls, but it also requires that any mental state we have is ultimately nothing more than a state of matter. This reduction of the mental to the physical is what the idea of a philosophical zombie is imagined to refute.

CONCEIVING OF A ZOMBIE

Let us imagine such zombies, then, and see what they can tell us about the nature of consciousness and other mental states. A zombie is to be conceived as a being that possesses all the same features that we do,

Philosophical Zombie Thought Experiment

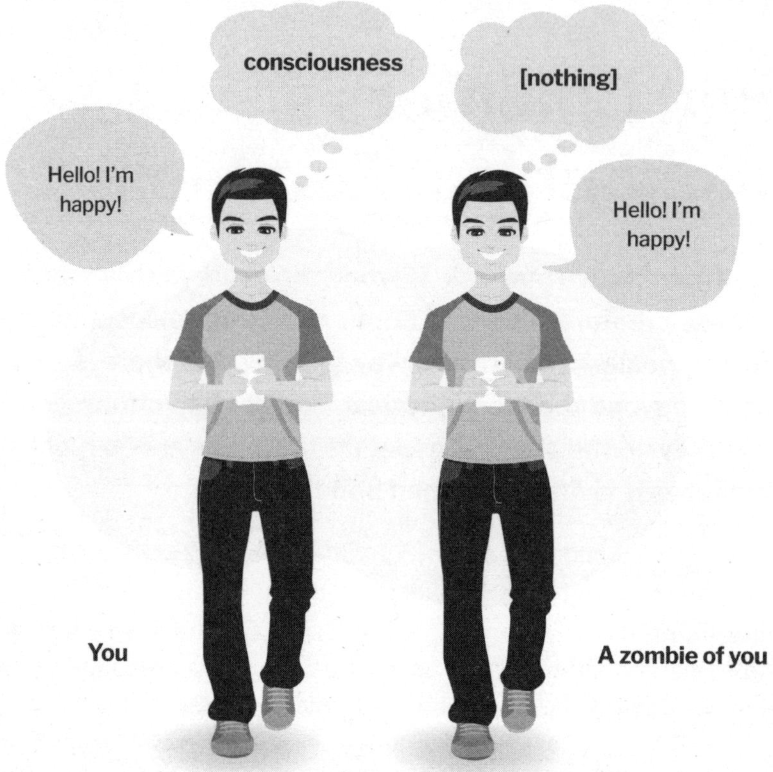

consciousness

[nothing]

Hello! I'm happy!

Hello! I'm happy!

You

A zombie of you

with a structure that is identical to ours, both biologically and physically. As we imagine this creature, it is important to be aware that this type of zombie differs from the Hollywood portrayal in that a philosophical zombie is physically identical to, and so indistinguishable from, other humans. If it is physically identical to other humans, how does a zombie differ from us? A zombie lacks all conscious experience.

David Chalmers (born 1966), building upon previous uses of zombies in philosophical literature, thinks the very fact that we can conjure up—that is, conceive of—zombies physically identical to us but without consciousness is evidence that materialism is false. An alternative way to say this is that if zombies are even possible, then materialism is false.

If it is not yet apparent how a philosophical zombie shows materialism to be false, the conclusion is made from the comparison of a normal human to a zombie. Let us personalize the zombie, as we have been asked to conceive of it, and make it physically exactly like you while lacking any kind of consciousness. It could even, allowing for mere appearances, act like you, talk like you, and behave like you while it lacks this consciousness, since these are all physical aspects of a human. All this being said, since you do possess consciousness, unlike the zombie, this means that there is something that belongs to your consciousness which does not belong to the zombie, and whatever this is must be something non-physical.

Crucial to this account is the unexpressed claim that a materialist thinks all conscious experience can be boiled down to physical or material conditions occurring in the brain, firing of synapses and other relevant neurochemistry. This would be an identification of consciousness with the material ordering of the human brain, nothing more and certainly nothing less. On Chalmers's view, there has to be some kind of account on offer from the materialists which will explain how a given arrangement of physical matter could give rise to conscious experience as we know it. He thinks that materialists are unable to move past this obstacle of explaining mental and experiential qualities about how we are aware of the world into purely physical facts about our bodies.

OBJECTIONS TO PHILOSOPHICAL ZOMBIES

Some have taken issue with this thought experiment, saying that it is impossible to conceive of a zombie physically identical to us in every way but lacking consciousness. These people forcefully maintain that if all the physical conditions about and in a body are the same as that of a normal human, then that zombie will also have consciousness as a human does. This follows, they claim, because consciousness is the result of physical biochemistry in the brain. A reinforced version of this same thought turns the tables on the zombie thought experiment. The idea of an "anti-zombie" shows, say its proponents, that we can conceive of a zombie with physical properties just like ours, which is also in possession of consciousness. Since we can conceive of anti-zombies, it would then be the case that philosophical zombies are impossible. At any rate, since the force of these thought experiments relies on someone being able to conceive of what their authors claim, and this act of conception by itself is used to claim victory, the easiest way to defuse the potency of the argument is to claim you cannot, in fact, conceive of what you are being asked to conceive.

SUPER-INTELLIGENT MICROSCOPIC BEINGS

If the argument for zombies, lacking consciousness but on every other count physically identical to us, is difficult to comprehend, consider another idea offered by Chalmers. Imagine that there is a group of superintelligent microscopic beings who invade your brain. These extremely little men proceed to replace all the neurological apparatus in your mind, not with electronics or machines but with their very persons. So instead of your brain operating with neurons you now have micro-men in their place, and these micro-men faithfully execute the exact same functions as the neurons they replaced, communicating with each other as neurons do. The question is whether such a network of men as neurons would be conscious? The suggestion is that you would think this collection is not conscious. It is difficult to decide. Could you conceive these micro-men to be conscious as a group?

The micro-men brain

Is the brain composed of
micro-men conscious as
the normal brain is?

Normal brain

**Brain with micro-men
instead of neurons**

41

Robert Nozick's Experience Machine

In his book *Anarchy, State, and Utopia*, Robert Nozick (1938–2002) set up a compelling thought experiment about our relationship and attitude to the very nature of reality. The details are easily comprehended. We are to imagine an *experience machine*.

Clever psychologists have invented this extraordinary device which precisely simulates reality, and all the while we are actually floating in a tank with electrodes attached to our heads.

By means of this setup, any manner of experience whatsoever is ours. We can have the experience of a professional athlete winning a championship or a painter creating an immortal masterpiece, or be present at the Circus Maximus in Ancient Rome as a spectator. Perhaps the most important detail of the experience machine setup is that you will not be aware that what you are having is merely a virtual experience. Unlike even the most immersive video game, you will not know you are in the machine. You will be experiencing pure satisfaction as long as you stay in the machine. Nozick's question, whether you would plug yourself in or not, has garnered the most philosophical attention.

WE SHOULD REFUSE THE EXPERIENCE MACHINE

Nozick thinks we should not opt for the experience machine. He discusses several reasons why we would choose not to plug in, or at least considerations for why the experience machine would be inferior to the life of reality. In framing the whole description of the experience machine, Nozick was careful to couch it in a very specific context. The important consideration he had in mind, making mention of it twice, is whether there is anything that we should take into account beyond what we experience "from the inside." If, after all, we ultimately value life only for the subjective experience we feel internally, it would be hard to turn down the experience machine.

THE REASONS WHY: EXPERIENCING VERSUS DOING

In his rejection of the experience machine, Nozick has several concerns. The first of these focuses on a distinction between experiencing and doing. We want to do an activity in order to experience the activity. He does not explain why this is the case, but taking it for granted that we do want the experiences along with the activities, we could ask why it is the case. Perhaps we think we are experiencing something only when we are doing it in or with our bodies in some relevant way. This explains why, when we dream of some grand adventure or see a film depicting something adventurous and wonderful, we do not think that we have actually experienced reality. Rather, we think that we have experienced something which represents reality in a diminished way. In a film or a dream, there is a sense in which we experience, but it falls short of the participation of an activity were we to perform it ourselves in the fullness of the actual world.

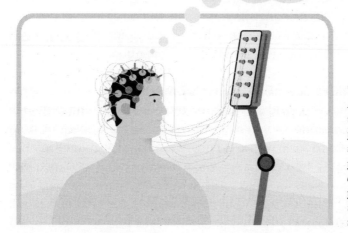

The Experience Machine: would you hook yourself up to a machine giving you amazing experiences, where you could not tell the difference from reality?

Objections to plugging into the experience machine

1 We want to experience by doing.

2 We would become a "floating blob" if we did so.

3 The experience machine is not real experience because it is preprogrammed, safe, unchallenging, and inauthentic.

THE REASONS WHY: THE MEANING OF PERSONHOOD

The second objection is that we value how we are as persons. Nozick thinks that there is a way in which we substantially cease to be persons if we plug in to the machine, because what we become at that moment is nothing more than a floating body in a tank. What defines and determines us is this "floating blob," rather than whatever it is we think we are experiencing, such as climbing Everest or exploring an unknown planet.

THE REASONS WHY: LIMITATION

The last concern has to do directly with the narrowness and limitations of the experience machine. One might think that an invention like the experience machine is boundary-expanding, since it opens up a limitless horizon of new experiences one can undergo. But this is not Nozick's assessment. In his view, since all our experiences are essentially determined by us, there is no contact beyond what happens to be of human concern. There is a limitation on a genuine interaction with the unknown and unexpected aspects of reality, which can be challenging, dangerous, and indifferent to our needs and wants as human creatures.

EXPERIENCE AND PLEASURE

Although he does not directly reference pleasure here, the experience machine has often been interpreted as an attempt by Nozick to refute a life centered on the pursuit of pleasure. In a later book Nozick brings up the experience machine again, and here he does equate the notion of happiness in this experience with pleasure. So pleasure is more directly in mind, since the idea of happiness as he uses it closely parallels the notion of internal experience in the experience machine.

In *The Examined Life*, Nozick ups the stakes by asking whether we would choose to be connected to the machine for the rest of our lives. In this slightly reformulated conception, Nozick thinks that there are other important factors for a human life outside the mere experience of happiness. One such factor is the qualitative life we are leading while we are happy. What he means by this is that if we lead a shallow life—for example, taking pleasure in mindless activities, like a mere animal—such a life is not to be preferred over a life of depth. This is in spite of the fact that in both situations we would equally experience the same sort of pleasure.

Because of this emphasis on a qualitative life, we think there is a kind of value in life in addition to the feelings of pleasure. Noting this, Nozick says we value not only our internal but also our external life. We think that how we live and the importance we give to it is informed to a large degree by the world we live in and by our interaction with that world. Our appreciation of how the world really is rather than how we want it to be shows that we value truth. In concluding, we could say that what the experience machine shows is that yes, we do want to experience happiness or pleasure, but we want it to be the result of a life lived in an imperfect world, not the perfect world of the imagination initiated by electrodes.

Robert Nozick believed that there is something in our relationship to the real world consisting of more than mere experience.

42

Thomas Nagel's Experience as a Bat

The provocatively named essay "What Is It Like to Be a Bat?" by Thomas Nagel (born 1937) is a thought experiment aimed at highlighting the entirely subjective nature of what it is to experience life from a given perspective. In a broader sense, it is an engagement of the mind and body problem—that is, an investigation of whether at its root the mind is nothing other than physical or must instead be explained by non-physical aspects, such as consciousness, which cannot be reduced to mere matter.

EXPERIENCE AS PHENOMENOLOGY

The account of what it means to experience something from a first-person perspective, from the vantage of an "I" navigating and interacting with the world, is explored in the philosophical field of *phenomenology*. Phenomenology, or what appears to oneself, is our experience of the world as we think and feel it. In the broadest sense, phenomenology is the totality of what it is like internally to live our lives as a reflection of the biological, psychological, and cultural influences that make us who we are. There is a distinction here between the objective world, which at least includes the physical, and our subjective state, taken to be our mental lives. As Nagel sees it, this suggests that mental phenomena, as they are experienced from a point of view, cannot wholly be explained in terms of what is merely physical.

WHY A BAT?

In order to bring this distinction out in more detail, Nagel asks us to consider the experience of a bat. He chooses a bat as his example because

Thomas Nagel asked whether we could even consider the experience of a bat.

he thinks that most people will grant that bats have experience—unlike, for instance, an insect. If bats have experience, this means "there is something it is like to be a bat." Bats present an interesting case, for they engage with their environment through echolocation, enabling them to determine shape, size, location, and speed by a means totally foreign to human experience. Their sonar is partly comprehensible by analogy to our sense of sight, but the utter exoticism of their ability makes this comparison doubtful.

More generally, Nagel emphasizes, he is not asking what it is like for me or you to be a bat, but what it is like for a bat to be a bat. He is not asking you to imagine a bat swapping bodies with you so that you can experience what it is to have bat-bodied experience. Rather it is an interest in how experience appears to the bat itself. Because we as humans do not possess the makeup, psychologically and neurologically, of a bat, it is theoretically impossible that we could experience what it is like to be a bat. We start, and for that matter, end, with how we think and experience as humans, and for that reason are ultimately restricted from experiencing the world as a bat does. This inability to understand what it is like to be a bat also gives us a reason to be careful in our own conceptions of the subjective states of other creatures, including humans. We should not make assumptions about the depth or shallowness of this experience on the one hand, while on the other we should acknowledge that there is a subjective life privately inhabited by the individual which is forever closed off from us. This is not merely because these experiences are hidden away from us, confined within the mysteries of that invisible and so indiscernible element we call thought. Rather, in principle we are doomed to fail to understand the experience of a bat because we are not a bat, equipped with all the necessary capacities to think and perceive as only a bat, and not a human, does.

EXPERIENCE IS NOT MATERIAL

One concern of Nagel is what he calls *psycho-physical reduction*. This is the project of identifying what are essentially psychological experiences with states of physical matter. On this view, states of the mind are really only arrangements of matter and can be properly understood as such. This scientific impulse, as productive as it can be, roots out the uniqueness of viewpoint where it can and replaces it with a conception of objectivity.

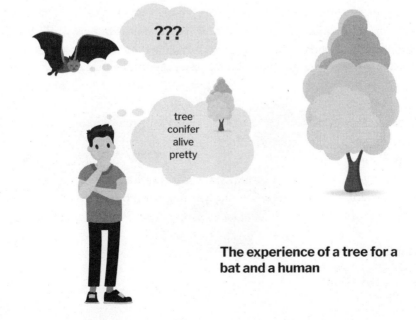

The experience of a tree for a bat and a human

Nagel's explanation of the subjective elements of the life of a bat serve as a critique of this materialism. Of course, there is nothing special in the example of the bat, as the explanation could equally apply to the inner life of any creature capable of experience. Any such creature's experience of the world cannot be explained only in terms of the objective features of matter, at least as our understanding of the physical universe stands. When we explain, or translate, what happens in the realm of experience into merely a physical understanding, we lose track of subjectivity—the very thing we are seeking to understand.

A serious implication of associating the mental events of experience with the physical is understanding what this even means. If mental events are simply physical events, there is some mystery in understanding how this could be. One route is to say that mental phenomena are caused by states of the brain—that is, by physical states. But even if we take this as true, how far does this go in informing us, in telling us something about mental states? Not very, it seems. The entire array of mental phenomena, from thoughts to emotions, could in theory be described in physical terms, but without any illumination as to what the content of that mind is. The pleasure felt by listening to a beautiful song or the imagination present in conceiving the plot to a novel could be described, some day, in terms of the firing of synapses and other chemical occurrences in the brain. But in terms of experiencing the pleasure of the song or the creative wellsprings of writing, these kinds of descriptions tell us nothing of what it is like to have them. At the close of his paper Nagel recognizes that this is a threat to the idea of physicalism. If it is true that matter is all there is, physicalism needs to find a way to recognize and explain subjective states in order to retain the quality of what it is like to be someone.

What it is like to be a bat is NOT to put yourself in the mind of a bat

43

Hegel's Thesis, Antithesis, and Synthesis

The history of dialectics is rich in the history of philosophy. In Ancient Greece a great tradition started with Plato of practicing philosophy as conversation, often with two interlocutors, as a shared enterprise to arrive at the truth.

The friction of these opposing sides is not merely to provide an opportunity for disagreement among the differing parties, but to advance by mutually informed criticism to a position of knowledge. G. W. F. Hegel (1770–1831) broadened this concept beyond the scope of two individuals, extending it to entire fields.

PLATO ON DIALECTIC

Although Hegel believed that dialectical practice was the heart of philosophy, he felt Plato's approach was seriously lacking in the way that disputed claims were resolved. There is an all-or-nothing aspect in the dialogues, Hegel thought, which blocked any road to progress. If some proposition were tested and found to be wanting, then the disputants would be dependent on some new candidate, forcing them to start from square one.

DIALECTIC IN HEGEL

Hegel's understanding of the proper science of dialectic, in which he envisions actual progress occurring, has been called *thesis/anthithesis/synthesis*. Although he did not himself use these Greek terms, this is a helpful and pithy characterization of this philosophical process. In sketch, thesis/antithesis/synthesis refers not to three parts but to three different consecutive stages in the formation of knowledge. The first stage, *thesis*, is that in which some theory or definition is posited, a determinate

Georg Friedrich Wilhelm Hegel took Platonic dialectic and altered it so that it was a constructive form of philosophical progress.

statement, idea, or claim. In the second stage of *antithesis*, the dialectical element presents itself. This stage is a moment of opposition compared to the first stage, which, as it were, merely offered up an uncontested idea. By contrast, the second stage causes the original statement in the first stage to enter into what is almost a self-contradiction. In the final and third stage, *synthesis*, there is a resolution of the opposition seen in the second stage. This resolution is characterized in different ways, but perhaps what is most important to understand is that the third stage is a recognition that something importantly new arises out of the contradiction seen in the second stage.

Thus the contradiction of the second stage is not merely a refutation of what has been claimed in the first stage; it is not a dead end but a starting point, or at least another link in a chain which will in turn have others

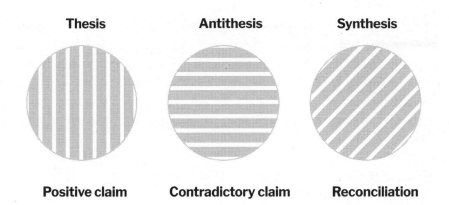

Thesis	Antithesis	Synthesis
Positive claim	Contradictory claim	Reconciliation

following it. The conclusion, if we can call it that, of this third stage is important for Hegel, not only in what it states but in the way in which the statement has been reached. For this reason, he often referred to this whole process as one of *determinate negation*. It is determinate in that a definite and positive result has come about; it is not a contradiction which ends in the total destruction of the original proposal. It is a negation, because although it is determinate and thus has content, this content is the result of a contradiction at the second stage.

BEING/NOTHINGNESS/BECOMING

All this may sound convincing, but it is still rather abstract. So before we look at an example, it is helpful to recognize that this abstraction serves a purpose. Hegel was describing the formation of all knowledge, so the process has to be broad enough to capture scenarios differing as widely as logic and history and philosophy. The most common example of thesis/antithesis/synthesis is being/nothingness/becoming. So if being is the positive statement, a simple assertive claim, then the opposite of being is nothing. This seems clear enough. Lastly then is the idea of becoming, which is not entirely being, existence, but it is not nothing either; coming to be represents both being and not being.

DIALECTIC AS A HOLISTIC PROCESS

One of the important takeaways from Hegel's account is an emphasis not necessarily on the end stage but on the process as a whole. Part of this owes to a recognition that it is the process itself which results in the final conclusion. But there is another element in the final stage, which is just as important. This is the belief that the final stage of synthesis contains within itself a "totality." Within the last stage is not merely some new product that was not there before. The last stage contains within itself the previous two stages. So there is a sense in which the last stage preserves what has gone on before, while at the same time displacing or supplanting it. We could say that the previous stages are recycled and refashioned in the synthesis. The benefit of this understanding is that negation does not stand by itself, resulting in an entirely refutative elimination of a thesis.

HEGEL'S VERSUS PLATO'S DIALECTIC

Hegel considered this triadic structure of dialectic as superior to the classical model of Plato in several different aspects. First, we can say that the "organic" expression of the synthesis arises from the previous two stages. A given thesis is not randomly dropped in and examined—like a definition of courage or piety for Plato—but is an idea able to be developed and honed. Secondly, the synthesis proceeds cumulatively by building upon what has been said earlier and transforming it into something new. Thirdly, this process is a genuine progress in that subsequent instances of synthesis are more comprehensive than prior ones. Lastly, this process is driven to a completion since what is the synthesis in one process can serve as the thesis in an entirely new process. In this new process, in turn, everything which has transpired is likewise preserved in the synthesis yet to come.

It is in the last idea of completion, verging on perfection, that we see Hegel's most popular idea extending to the sphere of history. The world is in a constant state of change, but each age has its own character, a *zeitgeist* sweeping it from the current paradigm to a new synthesis, a revolution bringing us to the current moment in history.

Example of Dialectic

 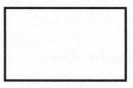 

Being   **Nothing**   **Becoming**

44

Newcomb's Paradox

Newcomb's Paradox, or Problem, is one of the more bizarre philosophical paradoxes, with interesting consequences for logic, decision theory, philosophy, and even theology. Although an analysis of a solution—if indeed there is one—becomes quite sophisticated, the problem itself begins rather simply. There are two boxes. You have to make a decision to pick what is found either in one box or in both of them.

THE SETUP OF NEWCOMB'S PARADOX

So far, this seems pretty easy, right? Just choose both boxes and if it turns out there is something undesirable, throw it in the rubbish. However, there are restrictions on your choice, and these significantly complicate the matter. To start with, one of the boxes is transparent and the other is not. So you can clearly see what is in one box, but not what is in the other. Things only get more intricate from here. There is $1,000 (or whatever currency you prefer) in the transparent box, and you can clearly see the stack of money lying there. Inside the opaque box are two possibilities. But since you cannot see what is there, you do not as yet know which. One of two things is there: either nothing at all or $1 million. What determines whether you get the fortune or nothing at all? This is where the strange element comes into the whole affair. Whether there is or is not $1 million inside the opaque box depends on what you will do. This is because there is an infallible being who predicts what you are going to choose. If this being predicts you will choose both boxes, the opaque box will contain nothing. However, if the being predicts you will choose only the single, transparent box with $1,000, it will place $1 million inside the opaque box.

PICK: ONE OR BOTH BOXES

With these conditions in place, which will you choose? One box with $1,000 or the two boxes together? Remember, this whole arrangement comes with the condition that if this knowledgeable being knows you will pick both boxes, then there will be no pile of $1 million. So which do you choose? An awareness of the predictive powers of this being might prompt you to choose only one box. After all, if you do pick both boxes, the being will have predicted you will choose this way and left the box empty. You would just be wasting your time by picking both boxes, the reasoning goes, because this being will have predicted that fact. So it is better to just pick the one box with $1,000.

An infallible being will put $1,000,000 in the second box if you choose only the $1,000 box, but if you choose both boxes, he will leave the second box empty. One box or two?

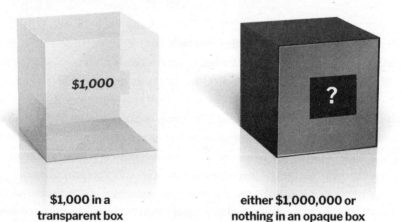

$1,000 in a
transparent box

either $1,000,000 or
nothing in an opaque box

THE APPEAL OF THE TWO CHOICES

But there is also a rational appeal to be made for choosing both boxes. Looking at both boxes, you think to yourself, "Either the money is there or it is not. My thinking or choosing this box could not possibly affect the contents of this box. Even if it turns out the money is not there, I will still get $1,000 from the other box. But if that $1 million's there, then all the better for me."

There is another "nothing to lose" perspective into which you could talk yourself. You could think of the one-box or two-box options as both resulting in $1,000. However, if you pick two boxes there is a kind of

Reasons for picking one or two boxes	
One box	Two boxes
If I pick two boxes, then the being will know that, and not place a million dollars in the second box, so it would be a waste of time to choose both boxes.	If I pick one box, then I'll miss out on what may be in the second box. True, it may be empty, but I have nothing to lose if it's empty.

wild-card element to the second box, in that it might have $1 million. If it does not, you still get $1,000 and this is not any worse than choosing the single box.

As it is formulated, people often have strong reactions to the paradox, and consequently a strong opinion on whether to take two boxes. Considered merely in terms of probability, it is more prudent to pick two boxes since this option maximizes the possibility that you will receive $1 million, while if you opt for the one box alone this guarantees the $1 million will not be yours. We might say that this option appeals to those who are primarily concerned with the monetary payout or who view the paradox from the position of a statistical problem.

Those who are drawn to the one-box solution are steadfastly attentive to the conditions of the setup, reasoning that it is foolish to try to subvert the knowledge of an infallible being who knows what choice we are going to make. An added wrinkle is that it is easy for people to exchange this being for a conception of God. Thus Newcomb's paradox takes on a theological complexity and shades into a moral problem as well—for who wishes to go afoul of the knowledge of God?

Although the theological interpretation of the paradox is probably wrong, it isolates one of the key factors in resolving this philosophical quandary—if indeed there is a solution. This has to do with the values or interpretive framework in which we understand the paradox. Which element of the paradox we choose to focus on can seemingly result in different recommended choices. If we focus on the omniscience of the infallible being, and appreciate its comprehensive knowledge of our future choice, we will choose one box, while if we focus on merely statistical likelihood and payout, we will be drawn to two boxes.

Maybe the most intriguing aspect of the paradox is what is happening in the opaque box. Is it or is it not holding $1 million at the time we decide to pick one or two boxes? If the box were translucent, what would we see? It's obvious that this would affect our choice dramatically, for if we saw $1 million, we presumably would go for two boxes. Or, do we suppose that even if the money is there, at the very moment we choose both boxes the infallible being causes the cash to disappear? This indicates that an important and hidden aspect of this thought experiment is the assumptions and interpretations we bring in attempting to resolve it.

45

Logical Positivism

Logical Positivism was a movement in the early twentieth century concerning the nature of knowledge, which widely influenced the practice of philosophy and logic. Also known as Logical Empiricism, the movement is best known now for its tenacious adherence to the principle of verification. This principle gives priority to the truth or falsity of statements, so that a proposition has meaning only if it is demonstrably and conclusively shown to be true, or on the other hand false. In positivism it is preferable that an alleged fact or assertion be proved false rather than being neither true nor false.

Because of adherence to this principle, entire areas of scholarly pursuit were deemed to be meaningless by the positivists, among them ethics, metaphysical claims, religious assertions of knowledge through revelation, and convictions arrived at through private intuitions. Metaphysics was such a disreputable field that A. J. Ayer (1910–89), considered one of the founders of this movement, said that David Hume's judgment "commit them to the flames" should be dutifully applied to all such speculative endeavors. Although not a formally organized group, many philosophical luminaries, such as Ludwig Wittgenstein (1889–1951) and Rudolph Carnap (1891–1970), gave support, in one way or another, to various aspects of this project throughout the first half of the last century. To a great many observers this movement helped to give rise to the current prevalence of what today is termed analytic philosophy.

THE POSITIVIST PROJECT

Characterizing it from a more positive standpoint of what it did stand for, rather than what it rejected, positivism sought to clarify and standardize knowledge through a common language available to all scientific pursuits. This concern emerges from a desire for language to represent the world—that is, words should refer to objects or states of affairs in the world. Because there is a world out there subject to the verification of our senses, we can match up the claims articulated in language about this world, in order to confirm or deny that what has been claimed is true or not. From the position of positivism, if an expression could neither be true nor false, nor empirically tested, it was considered not to have been said poorly or even incorrectly, but rather to be expressing nothing whatsoever. It would, and almost certainly must, say something about the mere feelings of the person uttering it, but as a statement it would be utter nonsense.

A. J. Ayer was an enormously influential philosopher in the twentieth century and a cornerstone of logical positivism.

LANGUAGE AS THE FOCUS OF PHILOSOPHY

More particularly, we may identify the project of positivism as a collection of several beliefs which are conceptually related and centered around the relationship that philosophy has to language and language has to the human endeavor of seeking knowledge. Along with finding a way to make language standard with the ultimate aim of precision, there was a flip side to this project, a necessity to reject as imprecise and meaningless any subject or assertion which could not be verified by a careful comparison with the world. This included the rejection of propositions containing certain unverifiable judgments, such as "No man is virtuous" or "Marriage is a beautiful thing." Because of its emphasis on precision and clarity, there was also an emphasis on transforming arguments into formal and logical statements, which could then be tested for truth or falsity with the utmost transparency. Resisting theoretical abstraction, positivists were eager to avoid the claims of generalizations, instead focusing relentless attention on the details of particular circumstances.

The value it placed on clarity meant that positivism was intensely

interested in the use of ordinary language. Part of this was an acknowledgement that the meaning of language is determined by how it is used. So it is only by focusing on the actual use of language that we can understand what is meant, and philosophical theories must often be measured and understood in light of the way in which the language is ordinarily employed.

The positivist pursuit of a language pure and applicable to the demands of a rigorous science led to the consideration that language can, at root, be reduced to certain elementary statements. These in turn concern what is happening in the world and so are theoretically and actually observable, verifiable, true or false. So even those statements designed to capture the most complex and sophisticated scientific theories are nevertheless reducible to observable events.

CHALLENGES TO POSITIVISM FROM WITHIN AND WITHOUT

Owing to the diffused nature of positivism, there were pressures from both within and outside the movement. The most significant of these, often described as the main cause of positivism's downfall, was aimed at the principle of verification itself. The objection to the principle is that it is not itself subject to verification by the senses. How can one verify the verification principle by appealing to empirical means? For this reason, many critics have thought that logical positivism was a doomed, self-contradictory enterprise from the beginning. Positivists have in turn replied that the verification principle was something akin to a convention or a tentative practical guide to further their investigative project, not an inviolable rule.

Another serious challenge was the formulation of universal laws of nature or physics. Individual instances which lead, by the force of accumulation, to positing a law can of course be verified, but the generalized law itself cannot be verified. The reason is that although each new further instance could reinforce the authority of the law, there could also be some rogue circumstance which could disprove the law. So while it might be true, given every example we have seen so far, that steel melts at a certain temperature, we cannot formulate this observation as a law because there might be some future instance of steel which could falsify it. Even under ideal laboratory settings where all variables are controlled for, it is theoretically possible for a given sample of steel to melt at some totally unexpected temperature. One solution to this problem, which proved controversial among positivists, was to say that a statement does not have to be verified in actuality but only has to be verifiable in principle. Needless to say, since the verification principle, which is at the core of positivism, brought significant difficulty, positivism itself did not, in a robust form, survive the century.

Scientific laws pose a challenge to the verification principle

Example: "Water boils at 100°C"

There may be some water somewhere that does *not* boil at 100°C. So either:

One must have knowledge of all water everywhere to state the law

Or the verification principle cannot account for scientific laws

46

The World as a Computer Simulation

Are we living inside a sophisticated computer program? This may sound like a hellish absurdity, but some philosophers and scientists believe that this is not only a possibility but likely. In the history of philosophy there have been many proposals as to how we could be or even are deceived about the fundamental nature of reality.

Plato offered up his famous Allegory of the Cave partially as a description of the deep and hidden ignorance we possess in our perception of reality. Descartes had doubts that an evil demon was causing all his thoughts and sensations for perverse amusement. Immanuel Kant divided reality into a phenomenal world of appearance and a noumenal world of things as they are in themselves, completely independent of how they appear to us. So reality as a grand illusion is not a new idea.

THE COMPUTER SIMULATION

The basic idea behind the computer simulation is that you are not merely immersed into a computer program, the way we say that a real person is plunged into the middle of a virtual reality computer game. The idea is more comprehensive, in that you yourself are part of the simulation: what you think is your body, your perceptions, your emotions, even your very thoughts as you read this have all been fashioned by the dictates of an intelligently conceived computer code.

THE PRECONDITIONS FOR A COMPUTER SIMULATION OF OUR WORLD

If all this is true, who created this computer simulation? Why? And most importantly, what is the argument or even evidence that any of

The world as a computer simulation

Advanced computer

The known universe

this is even possible? On the possibility of such a reality, we first need to consider what this grand illusion requires for its assumptions to be true. To begin with, in order for it to be possible for our minds to be nothing other than the processes of a computer, it has to be possible, at least in theory, for our minds to be modeled by a computer so that human minds could be reproduced or sufficiently imitated. The exactness and fidelity of creating these artificial minds would parallel the whole of human experience, for it would need to account for the complexity of consciousness. It would also need to reproduce an accurate experience of what we feel and perceive as a mind inside a human body, with its various interactions with different bodily parts and organs, and in general to offer a way of representing the pain and pleasure of the mind-in-body creatures that human beings are. Since the mind is not an empty vessel but is filled with all kinds of thoughts, beliefs, and desires about the outside world, any simulation that accurately models the mind would likewise be required to mirror the external world which forms the content of much of what the mind experiences.

THE SCOPE AND SOPHISTICATION OF THE SIMULATION

So if the mind is to be simulated, in a computer program or anywhere else, then the world must also be simulated if that simulation is to capture what our minds are like. Since both the mind and our world are enormously complicated, you may be thinking that any computer which

Could the vast sophistication of our universe be explained as the result of a computer code?

could effectively simulate these would be almost too incredible to imagine. It does indeed require a large leap of the imagination, but advocates of the simulation theory believe that it is not far-fetched. They point out the amazing rate in increase of the processing power of computers in the last few decades. One such example is Moore's Law. This says that the number of transistors on a microprocessor chip will double every two years, a prediction which has more or less held true for decades, with a parallel increase in computing power. Whether this incredible advance in technology will continue apace has yet to be determined, but it does not seem too absurd to think that in 50, 100, or 500 years in the future even the computing capacity of a common household computer will be far beyond anything we can fathom right now.

THE REALISM OF THE COMPUTER SIMULATION

As I have laid the groundwork for the argument, we must now remember what is probably the most important part of this setup—namely, that if a computer does in fact simulate a mind, then it is necessarily true that this mind would be unable to determine that it is merely the product of a computer program. This inability to distinguish between what might be a virtual mind or an actual mind plays into the experiment in the following way. Since in the framework of the simulation hypothesis we have already granted that it is possible for a sophisticated enough computer to simulate a mind, it follows that we might be simulations of a very specific kind. Future generations, with the requisite technology, could run simulations of their ancestors. This would be us. Another possibility is to imagine some alien race running simulations of their own, among which are civilizations with inferior technological advancement, such as ourselves. At any rate, in either of these scenarios, or in something like them, any society advanced enough to create a simulated world would likewise create many, many simulated people in these worlds. And perhaps they would even simulate many, many worlds, in turn exponentially increasing the number of simulated people as well.

THE STATISTICAL LIKELIHOOD THAT WE ARE A COMPUTER SIMULATION

The unpalatable consequence, if simulated worlds are possible, is that it is likely that you are one of these simulated minds. This owes to the fact that the number of simulated people would outnumber the number of real people, and that we have no way to determine if we are ourselves simulated or real. Since we cannot know if we are real or simulated, the odds are that we are simulated.

The simulation argument stands or falls on whether we think the mind is in principle capable of nearly exact duplication inside a supercomputer. But even the specter of this possibility raises important questions about existence and our ethical outlook. If one day as a society we are capable of creating a simulation with people, ought we to create it? If on the other hand, we are a simulation, how does that shape how we live our lives?

Grant that a computer powerful enough to recreate a human mind is possible.

Such a computer could just as easily create 10 trillion such minds as one, so simulated people would outnumber real people, and thus the odds are that you yourself are simulated.

| Simulated person | Simulated person | **Real person** | Simulated person | Simulated person | Simulated person |

47

The Riddle of Personal Identity

Personal identity is a mystery. We take it as one of the basic assumptions of our everyday experience that we are a person, and that the person we are is in a general sense the same person we were yesterday and the same person we will be tomorrow and into the indefinite future. But the basis for this assumption can be difficult to determine.

If we are a unity, what makes a person a human unity? Indeed, what is the subject of our selves? The body, the mind, the soul, something else, or a combination? The search for an answer to these questions suggests a concern, which is whether we can legitimately claim to be the same person, given the difficulty in identifying our personhood. If it turns out, for example, that we are to be identified with our material bodies, and our bodies change daily, and alter even more drastically over a period of years, then this brings into serious question whether the Kelly of age 10 or age 25 is the same Kelly spoken of at age 60. The issue of personal identity is for obvious reasons bound up intimately with the notion of personhood, and because it concerns the persistence of the self, this also has religious implications, touching on the existence of a soul and an afterlife.

THE IMPORTANCE OF PERSONAL IDENTITY

Of course, there is also a practical aspect: psychologically we take it for granted that we are the same person day in and day out. This explains why we both appeal to our memories of the past and aspire to good things yet to come, since we think the past and the future are ours by virtue of the fact that we are the same. So while it may seem that the question of personal identity is an exercise in needless speculation, minimally it

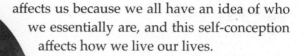

affects us because we all have an idea of who we essentially are, and this self-conception affects how we live our lives.

PEOPLE ARE ALWAYS CHANGING

Change in a person's life is hard to deny. Differences in our childhood and adult psychology and in the ageing and maturing process of the body are the most conspicuous, but there are also significant but overlooked changes such as shifts in ethical perspective, religious conversion, and the loss of formative memories. All of these changes affect who we are. Given the shifting nature of our persons, how do we explain who we are?

John Locke posited that the persistence of memory sufficed to ensure personal identity.

Given all the difficulties that we face in answering the questions above, one radical view is that there simply is no such thing as the self or person. Most people will hardly find this view appealing, but the idea is not to deny that we exist in a certain way. Rather, it is to assert that our idea of a person is a confused notion corresponding to no entity in reality. A closely related position holds that although we are not some single unity, we are a series of states or events in the brain relating to each other in such a way as to constitute what we label a *self*.

MEMORY AND PERSONHOOD

While acknowledging these uncommon views that deny the existence of the self, many thinkers are asking a theory of the self to offer an account of the persistence or continuity of our psychology. One of the earliest such accounts belongs to John Locke (1632–1704). His view was rather straightforward, identifying memory as that which accounts for who a person is. If you can retain the memory of an event or experience from the past from the perspective of the person who was actually living that life, then you are identical with that person.

Thomas Reid (1710–96) had a famous criticism of Locke's position, which appears to hit the mark. Reid asks us to imagine a brave officer in three different stages of his life. In the first we are to imagine that he is a small boy who misbehaves in school and receives a flogging. Later,

Reid's brave officer:
memory cannot be the basis of personal identity

1. The naughty boy who was flogged

2. The brave officer who was courageous

3. The brave man who was made a general

2 can remember being 1,
3 can remember being 2,
but 3 cannot remember being 1.

as a young officer on his first campaign this now physically mature man is able to perform an act of courage in battle. Lastly, as an old man, he is made a general. Reid now asks: what if the officer (at the second stage) is able to remember his episode of folly as a schoolboy, and the wise general (at the third stage) is able to recall his daring deed as a young officer but not his flogging as a boy? In Locke's view, says Reid, the boy is the young officer, and the young officer is the general, by virtue of sharing the relevant memory. But Locke's view also results in the odd consequence that the general is not the same as the boy, even though the young officer is the same person as both the boy and the general by virtue of sharing the same memory.

THE SPATIALLY EXTENDED CONCEPT OF PERSONHOOD
Others have conceived of the self as extending through time. On the face of it, this sounds quite odd. However, if one considers that we are spatially extended—one part of us, a foot, is in a shoe while another, our head, is in a hat—it makes sense that this could extend to time as well. Someone exists as a person on this understanding by extending through space as well as time.

Identity extended over time

Our bodies are extended over space:

arms at sides

head at top

torso in middle

feet at bottom

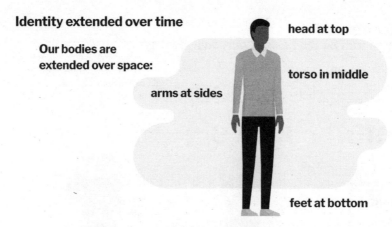

So our selves are extended over time:

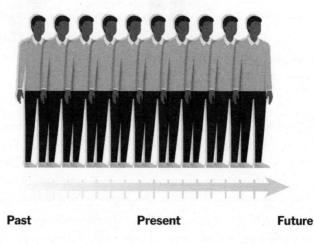

Past   **Present**   **Future**

THE SOUL AS PERSONHOOD

One of the more common approaches to personal identity is to identify the self with a soul. The existence and nature of a soul are controversial, but many people hold to a view which posits a soul inside our bodies. The soul is some immaterial substance, and there resides our mental life in general, and the center of our consciousness in particular. Precisely because the soul is immaterial, we conceive of it as immune to the kind of changes which could destroy the self if we identified the self with body alone. On this view the soul persists as a singular subject even while the body it is in, and the mental properties it possesses change and develop over time.

48
The Generation of Human Rights

To claim a human right is familiar enough to us today. Healthcare or a living wage or, more abstractly, freedoms such as the pursuit of happiness or the ability to express one's own convictions are all examples of what are commonly conceived, explicitly or not, as human rights. It is one thing to claim a right, and another thing to show that there is such a thing as a right, which others are obligated to observe, honor, and even enshrine into law.

There have been times when rights, and so the idea of rights, were not taken for granted as they are now. Today discussions often center around what concepts are worthy of being designated as a human right, but it is important to recognize that the idea of a human right had to be established in the first place.

COMMON FEATURES OF A HUMAN RIGHT

A human right has several elements. The practice of a right is considered, if not always, regularly inviolable. In addition to extending through all time, they are also extended to all people. So they are universal. Rights are the kinds of things that people have and exercise and that must be recognized by others. Most relevantly to contemporary situations, these rights are recognized formally in law. Because they are "human" rights, they do not belong to a person for being a citizen of a certain country or belonging to a certain group or having paid a fee to enjoy the privilege of the right. Human rights, if there are any at all, must apply to every human by virtue of simply being a human.

The French Declaration of the Rights of Man and the Citizen of 1789 is an early version of a document declaring human rights.

HUMAN RIGHTS AS REFLECTIVE OF DIVINE LAW

Before a right can become a law, or even a practice observed by a community, there has to be a reason why it has been adopted, or else it would never have been considered a right. Perhaps one of the earliest historical sources for the idea of a human right is the appeal to the divine. God has bestowed upon humans by virtue of their nature a law entitling them to a certain kind of treatment by other humans. In a society which believes in God or gods, or at least a government which seeks to enact laws that reflect the divine will, human rights are a basic feature of social life. Of course, for societies which do not believe in theological justification generally, other reasons will have to be given for how we come to human rights.

A LEGAL CONCEPTION OF HUMAN RIGHTS

One might object to the idea of God-given human rights because they are simply handed down, or claimed to be, without any explanation as to why they should be accepted. However, the creation of rights by fiat, delivered top-down, can also be seen in legal declarations of human rights. In fact, often legal documents do not even hide this fact and are called "declarations"—not as an effort to persuade but as an announcement about what has been decided and is being enacted. For example, one

Characteristics of a Human Right		
Universal	all times	
	all people	
Inviolable		
Often enshrined in law		
Thought to have a moral basis		

article in the European Convention on Human Rights states, "No one shall be held in slavery or servitude." Even if the abolition of slavery is agreed to be a good thing, there is no argument in the document explaining why we should think it good.

HUMAN RIGHTS AS BELIEFS HELD IN COMMON

It is granted by both religious and secular governments that human rights are a good thing, but how are we to justify their acceptance and enactment? One approach is to acknowledge the moral practices and beliefs that people through all societies have about human life. This is problematic for several reasons. It is difficult to discover aspects of human life which all societies can agree upon as the basis for human rights. Furthermore, the enactment of laws from shared morality can be tricky. If it is agreed by all humans that lying is bad, how should the form of a law reflect this? And what should the penalty be if someone does lie?

Nevertheless, forming human rights on the basis of morality, derived from religious sources or not, seems like a promising start. Rights can also be justified by aiming at the human good, or practical considerations, or need, or fairness or equality. Some of these appeals, such as to fairness or equality, depend on a pre-existing commitment to the justificatory principle itself. So if fairness is not something desirable by itself, or deemed justified as a good, it cannot serve in turn to justify a right.

WHICH RIGHTS ARE HUMAN RIGHTS?

There is a great deal of debate about what rights are human rights and how to ascertain this conclusion. The most controversial of these are rights that enter into the social sphere. Thus rights have been proposed

The human right to be free from slavery appeals to consensus.

for such things as education, food, and employment. On more solid ground are rights that are civil and political. These are rights such as freedom of expression and assembly, and the right to be free from torture. Non-discrimination laws can be conceived in some way as encapsulating an appeal to human rights, asserting that as individuals have rights by virtue of their common humanity, the rights accorded to this human nature cannot be forfeited by membership of an unpopular minority. Aware of these problems, human rights are often concerned with the rights of those who have historically been oppressed, abused, or maligned. Equality is stressed between the sexes, races, religions, and other common categorizations.

As good as we may think the spread of human rights to be, the idea is not without its critics. The longer the list of rights grows, the more disagreement there is about the merits of the rights included. Another worry is that the particular rights chosen reflect a small portion of the world. This is even extended to the concept of human rights itself. The concern is that a human right is a Western, industrialized concept foisted upon unwilling foreign cultures. However, whatever their merits or their justifications, human rights will be with us for a long time to come.

Various Justifications for Human Rights

Divine law	Shared morality	Equality	Practicality

49
Thought Experiments

Thought experiments are mental tools that have a long pedigree, dating back as least as far as Ancient Greece. Before discussing what all thought experiments have in common, let us consider a couple of examples, as this is probably an easier route to understanding what they are.

Thought experiments are to be found everywhere in philosophy. The most famous, and probably the most overused example, is the Trolley Problem. This is a moral dilemma involving a choice, either to allow a fast-moving trolley to continue uninterrupted on its present course, where it will kill five people tied to the track, or, by moving a lever, to divert the trolley to a side track, where it will run over only a single person.

THE MYTH OF GYGES
Plato (428–348 BCE) used thought experiments to plumb the depths of conceptually difficult problems, but also appealed to them when exploring the ethics of everyday life. In the myth of Gyges (GUYgeeze), a semi-historical figure named Gyges finds a ring that is able to confer invisibility. Plato asks how a just man, normally motivated to act justly because of the fear of harm to his reputation, would behave if he slipped on this invisible ring. In his view, the so-called just man would act as unjustly as the unjust man if he was motivated primarily by reputation, since the ring would ensure he could not be discovered in his crimes.

THE SPEAR THROWER AND ARISTOTLE
Another thought experiment comes from Ancient Rome, from the mind of Lucretius (99–55 BCE), defending the Epicurean idea that the universe is infinite. Consider, he says in a wonderful appeal to the imagination, that a man is standing at the end of the universe with a spear. When this man throws the spear, there are two possibilities as to what can happen. The

Plato's Ring of Gyges

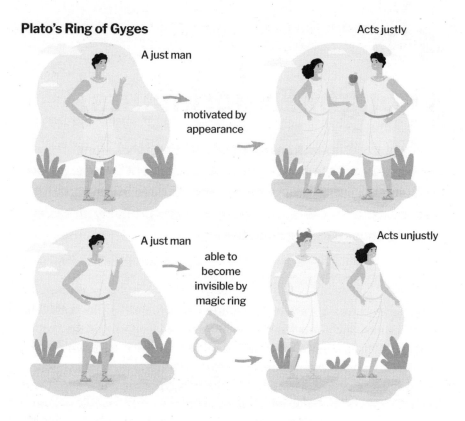

first is that the spear will pass the boundary of the universe, continuing on past the universe to something outside it. The alternative is that the spear will hit upon some wall or obstacle preventing it from reaching outside the universe. But this shows that there is something standing outside the universe. On either of these two options there exists something outside the universe, and Lucretius takes this as conclusive proof that the universe is endless and infinite. Aristotle (384–322 BCE) has an equally inventive thought experiment, also in the realm of cosmology. He asks us to imagine for a moment that the heavens stop moving, and now to think of the Earth. Where will the Earth move to, he asks, if heavenly motion is the source of the Earth staying in place (as he supposed)?

THE DISSIMILARITY OF THOUGHT EXPERIMENTS TO SCIENTIFIC EXPERIMENTS

Lucretius, Plato, and Aristotle take it that they are showing us something in these examples, and they are doing it by an appeal to our own ability to think of the situation described and to imagine the consequences of

Spear Argument for the Infinitude of the Universe

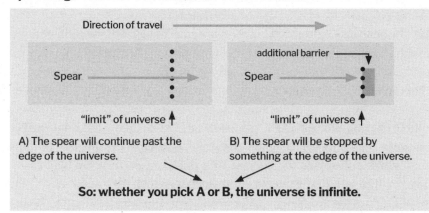

A) The spear will continue past the edge of the universe.

B) The spear will be stopped by something at the edge of the universe.

So: whether you pick A or B, the universe is infinite.

their imagined setup unfolding in an identical fashion as they claim. A potential discrepancy between the setup and what a philosopher claims will follow is one of the pitfalls of a thought experiment. Since we can never actually go to the edge of the universe and throw a spear, we are dependent upon our imagination not only for the experiment but for its supposed "findings."

The examples of Aristotle and Lucretius are a good comparison, since they are both discussing the nature of the universe. But Lucretius is rather clear on the terms of how his thought process is working, and what this shows about the finiteness of the universe, whereas it is unclear exactly how for Aristotle we are to imagine the earth's position shifting or why, and what the implications of this are. Thought experiments are often considered to be obvious to their proponents to such a degree that the authors confidently do not even tell us what the conclusion is!

The example of Lucretius does a nice job in bringing to our attention another facet of thought experiments. As the name suggests, they are meant to approximate or at least figuratively stand in for the kind of empirically based experiment one might find in the sciences. It is perhaps unsurprising given the scope in application of thought experiments—practically unlimited—that even science itself makes use of thought experiments, and these are indeed found in biology, mathematics, and economics, among other fields. In physics, for example, Isaac Newton made use of thought experiments, and there is evidence that Galileo used a thought experiment, and not the Tower of Pisa, to come to his conclusion that in a void all bodies fall at the same rate.

IMAGINATION IN THOUGHT EXPERIMENTS

Yet the scope of thought experiments again raises the question of what exactly they are and how to understand them. Their often intricate use of the imagination can also be used against them: skeptics are dubious that thought experiments show any manner of conclusion, and even more damning is the criticism that the answer they reach is precisely where the imagination of the philosopher directs them. The relationship between the fictional, imagined world of a thought experiment and the real world still raises the specter of a paradox even in the best cases. That is, it is odd that thought experiments, which take place not in the world but inside our minds, can nevertheless be successful in producing something true about the world that exists outside our heads.

There is a further question: is new—that is, completely novel— information added by a thought experiment, or does such an experiment conducted in the mind merely extract information already out there in the world? In these two possibilities we see two rival accounts of thought experiments. These accounts roughly break down into whether thought experiments are akin to insight or to argument. If they are more like insight, what happens is that someone conceiving a thought experiment gains an insight or perceives something about the way the world is, because the conceptual arrangement of the experiment has allowed

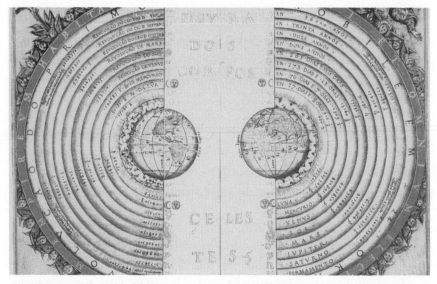

Aristotle's geocentric model of the heavens, as expanded by Ptolemy, was widely used during the Middle Ages.

this. On the other hand, if they are more like arguments, the way in which the experiment is presented is designed to show or make the case. Whatever the true nature of thought experiments, it is clear that they often provoke thought even if they do not always produce conviction. They can often serve as an attractive tool of persuasion because of their accessibility to our imagination.

50
Language and Thought

Ludwig Wittgenstein (1889–1951) once said, "The limits of language mean the limits of my world," and more famously observed, "What cannot be said we must pass over in silence." These two thoughts capture the spirit of the *Sapir-Whorf hypothesis*, even though Wittgenstein was not himself an adherent of the theory. The Sapir-Whorf hypothesis endorses the idea that language shapes the way we think every bit as much as our thinking affects the way we speak.

THE HYPOTHESIS EXPLAINED

The Sapir-Whorf hypothesis, also known as *linguistic relativity*, maintains that the way we think is conditioned or determined by the language we use.

It was named after two men, Edward Sapir (1884–1939) and Benjamin Whorf (1897–1941), whose ideas merged to form the theory as we know it today. There are at least two versions of the theory. The stronger version maintains that our thoughts are completely determined by the language we speak. Weaker versions allow that other factors besides language can account for our thoughts, or that, at minimum, thought has a level of independence from our language.

LANGUAGE AND THOUGHT

The reason the Sapir-Whorf hypothesis is known as linguistic relativity is that if the particular language we speak

Ludwig Wittgenstein believed that a chief aim of philosophy was to prevent us from being bewildered by words.

To not understand the language of a society is to be an alien

determines the way we think, then there are at least as many ways of thinking as there are languages. Each language has its own concepts, understanding, and framework in which thoughts emerge. Because of this emphasis, the Sapir-Whorf hypothesis has been taken to play up the differences between languages. In contrast, *Universal Grammar*, another theory of language introduced by Noam Chomsky (born 1928), asserts that there are structural features common to all languages.

COMMON EXPERIENCE AND SAPIR-WHORF

If we were to look at the world, evidence for the Sapir-Whorf hypothesis might easily be found. We tend to limit ourselves to discussions about which we have a vocabulary, and view those words outside of common experience as exotic and foreign to our understanding. When we look at treaties and relations among foreign countries, we may notice that countries which share a common language, such as the United Kingdom, United States, Canada, and Australia, have closer relations with each other than they do with non-English-speaking nations. If we go on holiday to some country whose language we are wholly unacquainted with, there is hardly a more alienating experience. Despite the commonality of shared human conditions, we are estranged from the social comforts of living among people who talk, and so think, like us. The Sapir-Whorf hypothesis says all these phenomena are not a coincidence.

THE CULTURAL MANIFESTATION OF LANGUAGE

Scenarios like those above bring into relief that languages are highly social. They are not only spoken and written in a social and political context, but they also arise in communities in essential ways. We are born and raised in a society, often with a single dominant language. Even the language itself changes over time and place. Consider the contrast in usage in highly urban or rural locations, or on different sides of the same country. The variety of different ways to express the English language partly accounts for why novels written by Charles Dickens about London are so different from Ernest Hemingway's novels about America.

DOES LANGUAGE DETERMINE OUR THOUGHTS?

So far, we have discussed one element of the Sapir-Whorf hypothesis, concerning how societies differ because the people possess different languages. But there is another aspect, the idea that languages in general are necessarily limited insofar as they are languages. If true, we are in some sense trapped by the languages we speak, since we are determined to speak only what language itself is able to articulate. In some ways, this is an even more frightening possibility than linguistic relativism. Since we do not know, and in principle cannot know, what the limits of language are, this brings the possibility of knowledge into question. There might be truths out there which language is unable to capture. The concepts cannot be expressed through language or are otherwise too strange. If Sapir-Whorf is true, it equally could be the case that the language we possess is able to tell us something about the truth, but not without warping or distorting the truth in the process. Imagine that truth or knowledge is like the fish in the ocean and language is like a net. If we go fishing, unknown and unseen to us, all fish smaller than the holes in our net will slip through. In the same way all the truths which cannot be expressed in language will escape our notice, just as these fish escape our net. The ultimate limitations of our language lie not in determining what it does say, but in what it cannot express.

LIMITATIONS OF SAPIR-WHORF

As mentioned, there are stronger and weaker versions of the hypothesis. As a strong statement about linguistic relativism, the hypothesis seems doomed. The existence of interpreters for live speech and translations for the written word are strong indications that thoughts can indeed be transferred rather easily from one language into another. At the very least it indicates that there is a sufficient level of similarity from one language to the next to accommodate regular conversation and the translation of literary material.

However, if we take the hypothesis to mean more modestly that what happens in the mind of a speaker of one language can never be reproduced exactly in the mind of a speaker of another language, there is probably some truth to this. An easy example is poetry, whose beauty is partly captured by the sonic form in which it is expressed. Even if the poem is translated in a beautiful way into a second language, it can never make the same impression in the way the original did. There appears to be some truth to the Sapir-Whorf hypothesis, although we can never know its full extent. One thing it should remind us is that the language and conceptual starting points for all of us differ, sometimes radically, and we should be accordingly patient and sympathetic in conversation not only with those from a different culture but even with those from our own.

Our language limits our understanding of what's in the world

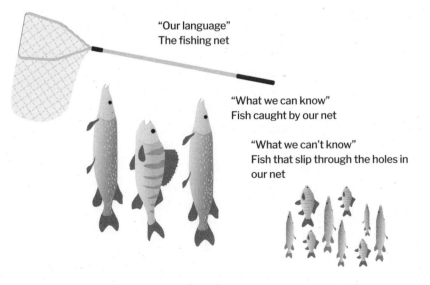

"Our language"
The fishing net

"What we can know"
Fish caught by our net

"What we can't know"
Fish that slip through the holes in our net

Index

Picture Credits

Alamy: 214

David Woodroffe: 31

Getty Images: 56, 92, 157, 163, 180, 194

Shutterstock: 13, 35, 44, 48, 52, 66, 87, 90, 91, 102, 110, 114, 121, 133, 147, 152 (x3), 164, 170, 171, 199, 208

Wellcome Collection: 18, 125, 135

Wikimedia Commons: 7, 22, 27, 39, 41, 63, 67, 73, 76, 82, 86, 95, 98, 106, 107, 115, 119, 127, 129, 136, 138, 139, 141, 143, 151, 154, 169, 182, 186, 202, 206, 212